The State of Housing D )23
Joint Center for H
of Harvard Univer

Edited by Sam Naylor, Daniel D'Oca, and Chris Herbert

The State of Housing Design
2023

Editors
Sam Naylor
Daniel D'Oca
Chris Herbert

JCHS Editor and Coordinator
Corinna Anderson

Research, Drawing, and Writing Team
Natalie Boverman
Emily Hsee
Sam Naylor
Lilly Saniel-Banrey
Aaron Smithson

Survey Analyst
Yona Chung

Copyeditor
Kelly Kramer

Faculty Research Advisor
Rahul Mehrotra

Design by Normal
Renata Graw
Lucas Reif
Anthony Randazzo

Design Support
Paul Zdon

Printed by die Keure

Typeset in Denim

Published by
Joint Center for Housing Studies
of Harvard University

Distributed by
Harvard University Press
Cambridge, Massachusetts

The Harvard Joint Center for Housing Studies strives to improve equitable access to decent, affordable homes in thriving communities. We conduct rigorous research to advance policy and practice, and we bring together diverse stakeholders to spark new ideas for addressing housing challenges. Through teaching and fellowships, we mentor and inspire the next generation of housing leaders.

jchs.harvard.edu

The views expressed in *The State of Housing Design 2023* do not necessarily represent the views of Harvard University, the Policy Advisory Board of the Joint Center for Housing Studies, or other sponsoring organizations.

ISBN-9780674294134

Content areas not indicated with an author
were collectively written, drawn, and
edited by the editing and research team.

More After Less
by Sarah M. Whiting

Harvard's Joint Center for Housing Studies has issued its signature report, *The State of the Nation's Housing*, annually for the past 35 years, documenting US housing trends and challenges. Across these decades, this report has become the benchmark for understanding this sector of the building market in this country. A consistent message across the most recent decade of these reports has been a sobering, comprehensive overview of high demand, low inventory, and skyrocketing costs, particularly for those Americans in the middle and below: renters, medium- to low-income households, and households of color. I am grateful to Dunlop Professor in Housing and Urbanization and Chair of the Graduate School of Design's Urban Planning and Design Department Rahul Mehrotra for asking what role design plays—or even *can* play—in this country, given the context that *The State of the Nation's Housing* has laid out year after year. In so doing, Mehrotra set into motion this parallel report that addresses the pulse and potential of US housing design. The pairing of these two reports is critical for grasping the give-and-take between policy and practice in this country. Illuminating what has been done with *less*, it is our hope that this report can point to how *more* might be made with, and for, housing in the future.

Comprising about 5 percent of the national GDP and about 50 percent of the construction market, housing is the largest building sector in the US, and yet it might well be the one that imposes the greatest constraints on design and innovation. Most of these constraints are economic and have been clearly identified in the Center's annual *State of the Nation's Housing* reports, including ever-tightening economic margins, escalating material costs, increasing demands, and greater general inequity across the country. Factors restricting design extend beyond the economic, however: two American propensities—the foregrounding of private property over collective life and the tendency to address conflict through litigation rather than social politics—have led over time to especially restrictive housing codes in this country. To wit, architectural licensing is dominated by health, safety, and welfare codes, rather than design expertise. In housing, these codes determine design decisions that range from door swings to banisters. Although the safety of our nation's babies is a justifiable concern, one might ask whether babies across the rest of the world—countries with less constrictive design standards—are truly in peril. In any case, it is a reality that in this country, economics, safety, and policy define housing. Certainly that focus ensures our collective safety, but this book reveals the extent to which *design*—the form and space of rooms, residences, and collective spaces; building densities, heights, and setbacks; and programming—can and *should* affect our country's collective life and future, in addition to all our safety standards and economic bottom lines.

Akin to the designers featured in this book, the editors—Sam Naylor, Daniel D'Oca, and Chris Herbert—have had to be especially nimble in addressing the elusive but critical topic of housing design. Rather than turn to those on the front line of pushing design—architects and academics—they elected to commission journalists and survey over 1,300 advocates, contractors, residents, developers, and designers, among others, recognizing that the value of design can be best seen by those in the field of everyday experience. Naylor, D'Oca, Herbert, and their team, including the book's graphic designers, Normal, present the information they gathered from this survey with remarkable graphics that clearly convey key points while consistently underscoring that this is a collection of opinions from a heterogeneous group of individuals, rather than a homogenized rubric of "information." These diagrams and captions capture *sentiment*. Although they do not coalesce into singular conclusions, certain themes emerge: a generally shared desire for smaller, more efficient living quarters; greater affordability; ecological sensitivity; and, finally, improved material and construction quality and durability.

These themes, which emerge from the experience and aspiration of American residents, find their design parallel in the 113 projects that demonstrate 25 themes that the authors have identified as design strategies that emerge from, or despite, the constraints posed upon this sector. Nine of these ideas are elaborated by invited writers, mostly journalists, who are especially adept at "translating" design for a broader public. As one of these writers, Mimi Zeiger, points out, most of the strategies in the book are characterized as being "stealth," "disguised," or "gentle"—in short, these strategies are under the radar, all suggesting new directions for how we live together in this country, on this planet, in more sustainable and more collective ways.

Over 75 years ago, German architect Ludwig Mies van der Rohe adopted the succinct motto "less is more" to describe his design approach. Leveraging loopholes within and/or drawing loops around existing constraints, the architectural projects and strategies in this *State of Housing Design* report show us how more *can* be done with the less that has been left to the nation's housing sector. But lots, lots more can be made if we, as a nation, put more into our housing sector. Read this book. Share it with your neighbors. Send it to your representatives. Bring it to your community's next design review meeting. Make a difference. Help us all put *more* into housing after letting it be reduced to so little, so *less*.

About This Book
by Chris Herbert

For over 35 years, *The State of the Nation's Housing* has been the Harvard Joint Center for Housing Studies' signature annual report. Reaching a broad audience from the public, private, and non-profit sectors, the report has become a vital reference that elevates both an understanding of and an appreciation for the fundamental importance of housing to the well-being of individuals and society.

Our annual report strives to be comprehensive, covering many drivers of the supply and demand for homes, trends in market conditions and housing policy, and implications for all segments of society and in all corners of the country. But, despite our aspiration to be comprehensive, we have paid little attention over the years to the physical buildings that are our homes, beyond examining structural inadequacies and energy-efficiency concerns.

And yet homes are fundamentally physical objects. Their design matters critically for how well they meet the needs of residents, how they enable or deter connections with neighbors, how economical they are to construct and operate, and how aesthetically pleasing they are, which can bring joy to those who experience them and exert a profound influence on the surrounding neighborhood's economic and social vibrancy.

The lack of attention to housing design in the Center's work is all the more glaring considering that the "Joint" in our name refers to our relationship with both the Harvard Kennedy School and the Graduate School of Design (GSD), where the Center formally resides. With this inaugural *The State of Housing Design* book the Center seeks to address this gap in our work, to live up to our aspiration to take a comprehensive view of housing, and to draw on design expertise at the GSD to call attention to the important role that design can and must play in addressing the housing challenges we face as a nation.

Rahul Mehrotra, the John T. Dunlop Professor in Housing and Urbanization, and a member of our Faculty Advisory Committee, provided the genesis for this book, recognizing the opportunity to leverage *The State of the Nation's Housing* report to focus on trends in housing design. Daniel D'Oca, chair of our Faculty Advisory Committee, was instrumental in bringing the project to fruition and in overseeing its development and execution. The project was led by Sam Naylor, a GSD alumnus and practicing architect, who gave form and life to the concept for the book. Corinna Anderson, the Center's Publications Coordinator, was instrumental in coordinating and editing the content. Much of the work was conducted by a dedicated team of current GSD students, including Natalie Boverman, Lilly Saniel-Banrey, Emily Hsee, Aaron Smithson, and Yona Chung.

Although the title *The State of Housing Design* is meant to evoke our signature annual report, this book is quite different in structure and approach. Where *The State of the Nation's Housing* is highly quantitative and aims to be objective, this book is by its nature qualitative and more subjective. But the two nonetheless share a common genealogy. Both are fundamentally concerned with identifying housing challenges and helping inform what can be done to address them. And both are intended to fulfill the Center's mission of advancing policy and practice to improve access to decent and affordable, sustainable homes in thriving communities.

For the Center's traditional audience, we hope this new work will uplift an understanding and appreciation of the critical role design plays in addressing the nation's housing challenges. At the same time, we hope it will introduce a new audience of designers to the Center's work.

What Is the State of Housing Design?
by Daniel D'Oca and Sam Naylor

What is the state of housing design in the US? What trends can we discern in the design of single- and multifamily housing? How are architects responding to the warming climate, the housing shortage and ensuing affordability crisis, and other major built environment-related challenges? These are some of the questions we asked ourselves two years ago, when we first identified the need for this book, which we hope fills a gap in the literature about contemporary housing. Although there is no shortage of publications that survey, analyze, and present the state of housing *policy* in the US—our sister report, *The State of the Nation's Housing*, being the best-known example—there are far fewer publications that survey housing *design* in the US in any comprehensive way. (Moreover, the surveys of contemporary housing design that do exist tend to overlook some of the quality housing that is being built today in this country.) Hence, this inaugural volume on the state of housing *design* in the US, which can be thought of as a qualitative companion to *The State of the Nation's Housing*. We hope to make this an ongoing series.

Broadly speaking, our focus for this book is on the new, novel, and notable. Our criteria for inclusion were never strictly defined but rather cooperatively negotiated among our editorial team, which included practicing architects, urban planners and designers, an economist, and six graduate students in the Harvard Graduate School of Design's MArch, MUP, and DDes programs. To identify projects, we made an initial long list that consisted of projects we knew, as well as ones suggested by colleagues. We subsequently distributed a survey to the Center's mailing list and to the Harvard Graduate School of Design that invited people to nominate new, novel, and notable projects for inclusion. (The survey, which received over 1,300 submissions, also asked respondents to identify themes, trends, and opinions on the state of housing design. These insights are summarized in a separate chapter.)

Although each of us had our own ideas about which projects on the long list counted as new, novel, and notable, we did collectively establish some criteria. First and foremost, to ground the book we chose to include only housing projects that were fully built and occupied in the past three years (roughly) and located in the US. The inclusion of young, mid-career, and established designers was also important, as was diverse race and gender representation. We also agreed to prioritize projects that had clear public benefits, either because they address critical environmental issues, achieve affordability in novel ways, respond to new demographic realities (for example, the demand for new domestic interior arrangements), or create or enhance public space. Many of the projects included in this volume thus confront what we believe to be the major built environment-related challenges of the day. More broadly, we sought projects that were in dialogue with influences we often think of as constraints and found meaningful ways to respond to things like enhanced guidelines for accessibility and resiliency and increased resident and community demands. Given that most of the projects included here are in relatively dense urban environments, many also respond creatively to oddly shaped lots, labyrinthine zoning codes, and community opposition. Indeed, another goal was to include projects from all over the country, in part to highlight the ways in which architects creatively navigate local building codes, climates, and other such "external" factors.

For these reasons, although a variety of residential types at varying levels of affordability were considered for inclusion, the kinds of stand-alone, high-end, single-family objects that adorn the pages of some of the glossier architecture publications—and that have the luxury of not having to grapple with many of the abovementioned factors—are not in abundance in this volume. Another goal was to ensure that the projects represent the multiple scales at which architects can innovate, from city block to shower curb, and to highlight projects that introduced scalable solutions. Estimates vary, but there is strong consensus that the US is short several million homes. While good design is always site-specific, the magnitude of the housing shortage means we must also deploy elements that can be repeated. Scalability is addressed most directly in our chapter on "Modular, Panelized, and Pre-Made" but scalable solutions for floodproofing, circulation, financing, and other elements can be found throughout. Lastly, we chose projects that could contribute critically to our understanding of contemporary urban character and architectural expression.

The resulting collection of 113 projects is therefore heterogeneous, despite whatever similarities astute readers might identify in the buildings' exterior expressions. Although they cannot be said to represent an exhaustive or comprehensive index of buildings, we do hope they offer a snapshot of the important work being done today in the US.

The book is organized around 25 themes prevalent in housing design today. For the most part, these themes emerged from the projects: only after we looked at our long list of new, novel, and notable projects that loosely matched the criteria above did we attempt to discern these themes. The themes are not all treated equally: nine major themes—along with their corresponding design projects—representing spatial, technological, and programmatic trends were identified early by our team and subsequently given as prompts to independent design journalists, who wrote essays that describe the theme, contextualize it, and offer examples of how it has influenced architectural expression. Smaller, somewhat more whimsical themes and trends are depicted in short graphic and textual vignettes that are interspersed between the essays.

A few caveats:

Buildings evolve. A dwelling isn't really ever completed; the end of construction is really just the building's beginning. How well does it meet the needs of its inhabitants? What impact does it have on neighborhood character, affordability, and resiliency? Does it produce co-benefits? Or does it merely benefit those who call it home? Evaluating buildings so soon after they are constructed therefore entails some guesswork, especially when post-occupancy studies are so few and far between. From this perspective, it's simply too soon to tell exactly how good the buildings selected for this volume are.

We might also point out that tying each of these projects to a distinct design theme is reductive, given how complex and multidimensional they are. This thematic organization also tends to ignore the political context in which the project was originally conceived: did the project have local support? What was there before it was built? What might have been built instead? How was it financed, and who benefited financially? In any built project there are winners and losers: who were they? This book is admittedly quiet on some of these questions.

Nonetheless, with this book, we hope we have elevated design work that pushes forward critically important social, environmental, and cultural themes. It remains our conviction that to design better homes and cities we need to understand the current state of housing design.

A Survey of Housing Design

Why not simply ask what people thought was happening in housing design?

From early August to late November 2022, we circulated a brief survey, with prompts meant to gauge general trends. We sent it to the Center's mailing list, then to the broader Harvard Graduate School of Design community. Our aim was to capture on-the-ground feedback from those actively designing, building, or shaping housing design in some way nationally.

We received over 1,300 unique responses from across 42 states and territories. Respondents hailed from Boston to Honolulu, from Cañon City, Colorado, to the town of Eagle Butte in South Dakota (population 1,258 in 2020). Gender demographics were split equally, with a majority-white respondent base. Most were mid- to late-career practitioners with the job title of designer, advocate, or developer, although many checked multiple boxes.

The survey intended both to inform the framing of the publication and to gut-check our early assumptions on emerging design trends. There was a healthy overlap between the themes that emerged in the responses and those that were taking shape in our research: respondents were—like us—keen to talk about sustainability, family-sized units, zoning, density, and affordability. However, there was also a level of disconnect between the kinds of work people told us about and the kinds of work we ended up focusing on in the book. This was evident in the large number of responses related to single-family and low-density developments—typologies that produce a large amount of housing nationally but that are not represented proportionally by the projects we feature in the book.

What's clear is that almost everyone is very concerned with the state of housing; generally, respondents wrote in animated language that we build too little, for too high a cost, and with not enough care. This section gives an overview of the survey itself, dissecting each question we asked, followed by selected quotes of respondents.

Experience Level
Percentage of total respondents

- No Experience
- Entry Level
- Early-Career 10%
- Management/Leadership 28%
- 23%
- Mid-Career
- 35%
- Late-Career/Expert

Primary Role/Job in Housing Production
Relative frequency of roles by respondents

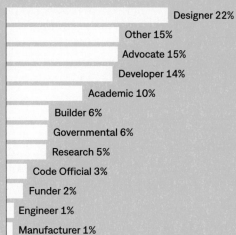

- Designer 22%
- Other 15%
- Advocate 15%
- Developer 14%
- Academic 10%
- Builder 6%
- Governmental 6%
- Research 5%
- Code Official 3%
- Funder 2%
- Engineer 1%
- Manufacturer 1%

States Where Respondents Work

- ☐ States with responses
- ■ States with 2% or greater representation

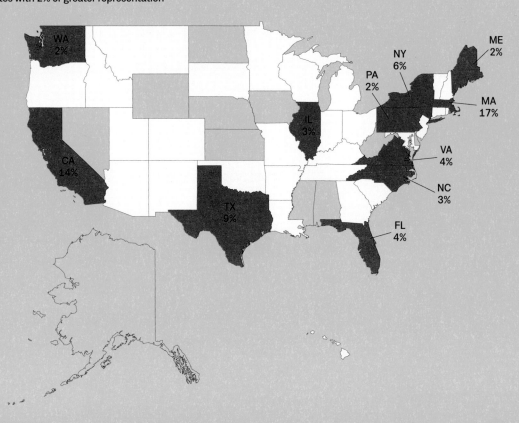

WA 2%
ME 2%
NY 6%
PA 2%
MA 17%
VA 4%
IL 3%
CA 14%
NC 3%
TX 9%
FL 4%

In the last two years, what design ideas have you noticed the most in newly built housing?

Smaller
All Electric
Affordable
Modular
3D-Printed
5-Over-1s
Micro
Open
Home Offices
Large
Multi-Materials
Highly Efficient
Luxury
Adaptive Reuse

Alternate Energy
4/5 Stories
Age in Place
Higher Density
Timber
ADUs
Accessible
Passive
Expensive
Tiny
Wood
Modern
Amenity Spaces
For Families

The above list represents the most commonly mentioned topics in order of response frequency. The highlighted topics on size and density are what we heard most about.

Here is what we heard about:
Size and Density

Code Official in Montana	"Smaller living space but more storage space."
Academic/Advocate/ Builder/Designer in Massachusetts	"Lack of verticality, acquiescence to neighborhood groups, even for projects at the periphery of neighborhoods and commercial districts."
Advocate in North Carolina	"The designs here in Raleigh, North Carolina, are more Miami-esque, meaning, they are tall/narrow in stature, built on small tracts of land, typically have a lot of natural lighting."
Designer in California	"Out of scale, malproportioned, out of context with surrounding neighborhoods."
Academic/Designer in Oregon	"Smaller residences, tiny houses, clustered developments and townhouses."
Academic/Researcher in Georgia	"Prefabricated structures sited in smaller infill lots."
Academic/ Designer/Developer in California	"In San Diego Co-Housing, multiple tenants share a space with one kitchen and living room. In some configurations, each bedroom has its own bathroom and main entrance, and the shared kitchen and living areas are centrally located."

In your industry or role, what do you see as the biggest external factors to building well-designed (as you define it) housing?

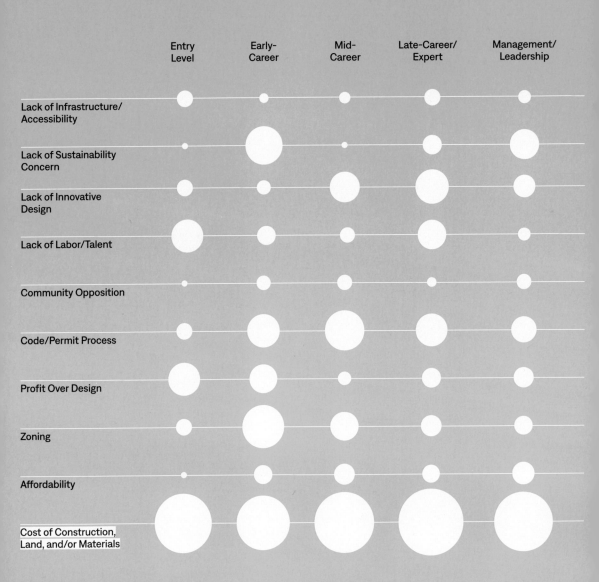

The above graphic of circles represents the relative density of responses grouped by thematic topic and organized by respondents' experience level. Cost is highlighted as the topic we heard most about.

Here is what we heard about:

Cost

Entry-Level	"Simply the cost. I am in a legacy Rust Belt city. It is hard to pencil out projects from the private sector, let alone with public funding. I would add that zoning and the regulatory process of getting a project approved from local municipalities incur unnecessary costs and wait times to the pre-development process."
Early-Career	"'Luxury' focus—often high-rise. Inequitable focus—gentrification and displacement; innovations are reserved for the most privileged; those displaced are the most distanced from well-designed housing."
Mid-Career	"Forgetting that middle- and low-income people exist; catering construction and design only to the superrich."
Late-Career	"There is a lack of government funds to build deed-restricted, high-quality affordable housing."
Management/ Leadership	"Cost of housing—builders have to rethink the 1,400-square-foot home (which was 40 percent of new construction in the 1980s; only 7 percent now) for affordability with much increased functionality."

What is missing most from housing design today?

If you could change one thing to enable better design in housing, what would it be?

Affordability
Renewable Energy and Efficiency
Knowledgeable Partners
Resilience and Green Infrastructure
Feasible and Cost-Efficient Design
Design Guidelines
Variety
Quality Building Materials
Original Designs
Joy
Bike Parking
Connection to Outdoor Green Space
Effective Renovation Strategies
Demographic Flexibility in Units
Design-Build Partnerships
Contextual and Scalar Designs
A Sense of Community
Skilled Labor
Collective Models of Ownership
Wider Range of Typologies
Density
Open Competitions
People's Life and Histories
Mix of Income Levels
Family or 3/4 Bedroom Apartments
Willingness to Make Less Profit
Up-to-Date Building Codes
Material Sensoriality and Details
Focus on Equity
Accessible Entries and Units
Character

Restrictive Zoning and By-Right Housing
Onerous Design Guidelines
Spatial Flexibility Over Time
More Open Space
More Renewable-Energy Incentives
Cooperative Buying Power
Access to Multimodal Transportation
Increased Density
Remote Work Areas
Accessible Bathrooms
More Durable and Sustainable Materials
Give Design a Soul
Make Rehab Easier/Cost-Effective
Speed Up Construction
More Natural Light
Engage Youth in Design Thinking
Encourage Passive Energy Systems
Cultural Understanding of the
    American Dream
Designers Who Engage the Community
Acceptance of Smaller Homes
Developer Commitment
Publicly Fund Housing R&D
Encourage Youth in the Trades
Two Means of Egress Rule
Broader National Building Standards
Non-Vinyl Flooring
More Architects Designing Housing
Public Typical Drawings/Details
Education of Regulators
Efficient Municipal/Community Review

The above lists plot the terms we heard most in each category.
Highlighted terms related to zoning were the most commonly
mentioned in response to the second question.

Here is what we heard about:

Zoning

Other	"By-right housing—put simple parameters on the design and zoning, let people innovate, and require engagement with residents, neighborhood, etc."
Academic/ Advocate Builder/ Designer	"[Establish a] clear agenda stated from the City of Boston as to what its goals are, instead of us having to discover them in the process of applying for building permits."
Developer	"The regulatory approval process is taking two to three years in the Seattle region. That is really affecting our ability to increase the housing supply. Also, cost pressures remove the ability to try new enhancements or extras."
Designer	"Probably regulations around zoning allowing for and/or incentivizing densification in suburbs and exurbs. Also, it's imperative that cities continue to be able to require developers to do public improvements."
Advocate/Designer/ Researcher	"Legalize point access blocks to 6–10 stories, to unlock small- and medium-sized mid-rise projects in more of the city. This is the backbone of cities the world over, outside the US and Canada."
Builder	"Planning codes and planners should want to be able to approve projects that don't all look the same and should be allowed and/or mandated to deviate from time to time—for sheer boredom of the architecture's sake and the jumbled city masses they are producing. All repetitive."

In the last two years, what small trends or peculiar details have you noticed in new housing?

Northwest region:
Black Trim
Bright White
Clerestory Window
Courtyard
Fancy Amenities
Gray
Indoor-Outdoor Living
Material Reuse
Perforated Metal
Podium
Shiplap Walls
Sloped Roof
Snout House
Stone Veneer
Superblock
Round Window

North Central region:
Black and Gray
Bright Colors
Brass and Bronze
Flex Space
High Ceiling
Large Bath
Open Kitchen
Metal Roof
Metal Siding
Tall Window
Vinyl Window
Vinyl Siding
White Block

South Central region:
3D Printing
Barn Doors
Blue/Silver/Brown/Gray
Coworking
Fake Bronze Hardware
Fireplace
Glass
Gray
Gym
Hidden Door
Live-Work
Metal Stud
Synthetic Material
Tall Roof
Urban Farms
White Painted Brick
White Wall Black Trim

Southeast region:
Black and White
Colored Panel
Cheap Material
Dark Shutter
Ensuite Bathroom
European Window
Fiber-cement Panel
Glass and Metal
High Density
High-end Amenities
Modern Farmhouse
Multifamily
Pet Amenities
Shallower Unit
Slab Home
Vinyl Siding
Wood Composite Material

Across all regions, people told us most about fake materials, prefabrication, modular buildings, outdoor spaces, mass timber construction, home offices, smaller spaces, higher density, sustainable features, and repetitive designs. The graphic above illustrates the various responses we received across country organized by region and alphabetically; and highlights the topic we heard the most about: materiality.

Here is what we heard about:

Materiality

Baton Rouge, Louisiana	"The use of synthetic cladding materials masquerading as something else—tile and plastics faking as wood, cladding misleading people to be wood that never needs painting, etc. The falsehood of materials."
Washington, DC and Arlington, Virginia	"More glass and metal, less stone/brick."
California	"Many times, clients, contractors, peers want to use materials that are recycled or certified but aren't durable physically or have a versatility of use (can't be refinished, will go out of style quickly...etc.)."
St. Louis, Missouri	"The use of black and gray colors on everything."
Santa Fe County, New Mexico	"Subway tiles. Barn doors. Fake-rock facades. Roof beams in all directions."
Columbus, Ohio	"Mr. Potato Head housing. Overuse of craftsman elements: board and batten, standing-seam metal roofs, etc."
Cambridge, Massachusetts	"I see lots of large, single-family homes that are white, neocolonial style with black windows."

Disguised Density

Not enough housing is being built across the country, period. Housing density—the number of individuals per unit in a geographic area—is still far below what could be supported by local infrastructure in most opportunity areas (close to transit, jobs, and services). Housing supply must be increased in lower-density areas to avoid more sprawl or greenfield development, which have well-documented negative environmental, economic and social effects. However, accompanying increases in height, street frontage, and building agglomerations can clash with collective perceptions of neighborhood character. NIMBY ("not in my back yard") opposition to development often foregrounds these concerns as part of a national debate on how best to accommodate more homes in the same space. "Disguised density" refers to a design strategy that many projects use to obfuscate their unit count with architectural moves that fit more closely with established local residential typologies. For example, this includes duplexes with one front door, townhomes squished to the rear of the lot, and apartments with far fewer visible windows. Entrances are hidden, surroundings are mimicked, and parking is shrouded. Although many of these design methods are well established, concealing density may come at the cost of creating a fantasy world of urban stasis. We highlight projects built on this knife's edge of a cultural battle—creating compelling character within the tight constraints of neighborhood and market demands.

In the US, where overcoming single-family zoning is still the prevailing regulatory hurdle, these projects exemplify the contemporary compromises involved in adding density where the status quo rejects it. Notable projects in Los Angeles, Seattle, Greenville, and Boston blend local vernaculars with novel urban form-making. Of particular note in the past few years was an open design competition[i] organized by the Los Angeles Mayor's Office and the city's Chief Design Officer, which generated new typologies of low-rise density. Entries blended international precedents with local lot dimensions and integrated home-grown American types with new policies.[ii] In the following essay, Mimi Zeiger breaks down these concepts, outlines several projects, and explores what this trend means for density in American cities.

i   "Low-Rise: Housing Ideas for Los Angeles," https://lowrise.la/.
ii See also: "Come Home Chicago: Missing Middle Infill Housing Competition," https://www.architecture.org/learn/resources/come-home/.

by Mimi Zeiger

In 2016, architect Barbara Bestor used the term "stealth density" to describe a multifamily residential development that her firm, Bestor Architecture, designed in Los Angeles's Echo Park. The neighborhood, historically a mix of Latinx families and bohemian artists and writers, was slowly, then very rapidly, gentrifying in LA's overheated housing market. Any new construction was bound to be suspect—both as a harbinger of displacement and disruption of the old, streetcar-era urban fabric. Although the term "stealth" conveys a contextually sensitive approach, a way to fit into an existing condition, it also reflects the anxieties of a neighborhood in transition. Changing a neighborhood's physical character threatens both longtime and recent residents.

Bestor drew inspiration from the modest single-family homes and occasional low-rise courtyard apartment buildings that line Echo Park's hilly streets. Named Blackbirds, Bestor's complex combines these two typologies to organize a series of duplexes and triplexes around a central parking court. Each building *stealthily* resembles a single-family home; the design uses pitched roofs and exterior paint color to break up the bulk of larger volumes, so new construction blends into the surrounding scale. "Two free-standing houses are connected by flashing, and the roofline creates the illusion of one house mass," Bestor explained to the online publication Dezeen. "Three houses, whose separation is masked, has the illusion of being two houses."[1]

1   "Bestor Architecture Uses 'Stealth Density' at Blackbirds Housing in Los Angeles," https://www.dezeen.com/2016/09/28/bestor-architecture-blackbirds-housing-stealth-density-echo-park-los-angeles/.

Stealth density is just one possible expression of this strategy. The editors of this book chose "disguised density," and a 2019 Brookings Institution report used the term "gentle density" to argue that replacing detached single-family houses with more homes on a lot could help reduce housing prices in desirable locations without disrupting the neighborhood. This "missing middle" between the stand-alone home and the dreaded apartment tower takes the form of multifamily townhouses, duplexes, and semi-detached structures packed tightly on a lot. "Building more housing on single-family parcels doesn't require skyscrapers," noted the report's authors, Alex Baca, Patrick McAnaney, and Jenny Schuetz.[2]

2   "'Gentle' Density Can Save Our Neighborhoods," https://www.brookings.edu/research/gentle-density-can-save-our-neighborhoods/.

Stealth. Disguised. Gentle. With each, language is used to deflect the fears and misconceptions that have accumulated around multifamily housing—biases that align multiunit buildings with the past specters of bleak public housing projects. That new development must slip quietly into a neighborhood underlines the long-held entitlement of home ownership and bias of single-family zoning. The Brookings

Viewed from above, the buildings of Bestor Architecture's 18-unit Blackbirds housing complex resemble single-family homes.

Institution report, for example, notes that Washington, DC, requires special permission for higher density in areas zoned single-family. Zeroing in on zoning-code terminology, the report identifies how the language of the code privileges low-density to "protect [single-family] areas from invasion by denser types of residential development." Words like "protect" and "invasion" suggest that code is weaponized against outside threats. Indeed, the report's authors stress that "'protection' entrenches economic and racial segregation."[3]

3   Ibid.

Both Blackbirds and Lorcan O'Herlihy Architects' (LOHA) multifamily housing development, Canyon Drive, follow City of Los Angeles policy guidelines. The Small Lot Subdivision Ordinance, first adopted by the city in 2005 and amended in 2016, was touted as a solution to increase affordability in a tight market via infill housing. The ordinance included reduced setback requirements and lot sizes. Building more units—in the form of detached townhouses—on a lot zoned multifamily or commercial was meant to target first-time homebuyers, although it is arguable if this plan was truly successful. In early 2022, two-bedroom, two-bath units at Canyon Drive were sold for around $1.4 million each. Although the price is conceivably less than a ground-up, single-family home on the same lot, the units sold for considerably more than the $1 million average home price in Los Angeles.

The authors of the ordinance recognized that increased density and potentially bulky massing indicative of multifamily housing would set off alarms, so a series of design guidelines dictates specific articulations of facades, entryways, and rooflines to prevent blank and boxy edifices ill-suited to the surrounding context. At Canyon Drive, for example, each unit has a unique identity. LOHA inflected the roofs of the townhouses so that each facade resembles a mid-century-modern A-frame perched atop the garage podium.

4   "$224K Grant from Planters Bank and Trust and FHLB Dallas Creates 42 Homes," https://www.businesswire.com/news/home/20180615005840/en/224K-Grant-from-Planters-Bank-and-Trust-and-FHLB-Dallas-Creates-42-Homes.

Similarly, in Greenville, Mississippi, the pitched roofs and shaded front porches that characterize the 42 townhouses of The Reserves at Gray Park suggest that individuation is neither simply an appeasement to NIMBYs nor a market strategy, but also a way of establishing identity and dignity for residents. Composed of one-, two-, and three-bedroom units, the affordable housing project by Duvall Decker with the Greater Greenville Housing and Revitalization Association serves low- and very-low-income renters. It's the city's largest single-unit housing development in more than 30 years.[4] Here, disguised density works to deflect the stigma historically associated with affordable housing, while demonstrating that an alternative to a detached single-family home might offer more than the suburban ideal. What if the American Dream was not about individual ownership and a green front lawn but, as illustrated at The Reserves at Gray Park, found in shared public spaces designed to foster community interaction and sustainable site planning?

The multiunit buildings of the Blackbirds complex cluster around a shared courtyard and parking area.

The inflected roofs of the townhouses in Lorcan O'Herlihy Architects' Canyon Drive project are designed to evoke the A-frame home designs that were popular in the mid-twentieth century.

5   "Construction of Santa Monica Apartment Building Appealed," https://www.surfsantamonica.com/ssm_site/the_lookout/news/News-2015/January-2015/01_23_2015_Construction_of_Santa_Monica_Apartment_%20Building_%20Appealed.html.

In many ways, disguised density is a study of aesthetics and perception: both a design exercise in vernacular typologies and a strategic game of hide-and-seek. But camouflage can't always ward off NIMBY critiques. Opponents of the Ashland Apartments in Santa Monica accused Koning Eizenberg Architecture of "shoe-horning too much building into the site" and brought concerns about increased traffic to Santa Monica's Architectural Review Board.[5] The opponents were large neighbors—Santa Monica homeowners concerned about the project's direct impact on their quality of life and property values. Considered a "preferred project" by the City of Santa Monica, the 10-unit development on a terraced hillside reflects higher density than normally allowed under code but was given an exception to incentivize more family housing to the area. Studios and two- and three-bedroom apartments are divided among four structures. According to the architects, the project achieves a density of 30 units/acre by bridging scales between a residential neighborhood (the source of the complaints) and a high-density, mixed-use development along Lincoln Boulevard to the west.

In 2019, the same year that Ashland Apartments opened, *Architecture Australia* ran an article about architects Hank Koning and Julie Eizenberg, describing their work as "smart, generous and empathetic,"[6] which is best embodied at Ashland in the abundance of private and shared outdoor spaces that allow residents room to socialize and take advantage of Southern California indoor-outdoor living.

6   "'Smart, Generous and Empathetic': The Housing Projects of Koning Eizenberg Architecture," https://architectureau.com/articles/hank-koning-and-julie-eizenberg/.

Ashland Apartments sits on a previously unbuilt lot in the center of the block and is edged on three sides by the backyards of adjacent properties. With no street frontage of its own, the other houses in this highly desirable neighborhood mask its overall density. A long, narrow (and contentious) driveway connects from the curb to the underground parking lot. The multiyear clash was, literally, a skirmish over "not in my backyard."

Although density triggers fears of "too big," "too much," or "invasive," at the heart of these kinds of fights is a battle over the continued viability of single-family zoning in neighborhoods, cities, and states where homelessness is on the rise, affordable housing is out of reach, and sprawl is no longer an option. As a paradigm, single-family zoning was built on pastoral fantasies and systems of social and racial exclusion. Bursting the fever dream of individual homeownership and the loose-fit urbanism it produces is bound to provoke conflict. During an event hosted by Laboratory for Suburbia that questioned what "house" means—both as a spatial product and as home—Gustavo Arellano, an Orange County–based journalist who writes on issues of politics, race, and suburbia, suggested we shatter our collective intoxication, using language that verges on revolution. "[I have to] throw this rock

An aerial image shows the change in density between the low-density suburban context of Greenville, Mississippi, and the townhouses of The Reserves at Gray Park.

Although The Outpost appears larger than its single-family neighbors, the building conceals an experimental approach to multifamily living.

Disguised Density

Koning Eizenberg Architecture distributed 10 units across four free-standing buildings at the Ashland Apartments, allowing patios and communal walkways to fill the spaces in between.

into the windows of the dream I have, and other people have, about where we're at right now" he said, holding up a painted rock from his childhood.[7]

7   "Sprawl Session 3: House as Crisis," https://laboratoryforsuburbia.site/SS3.

The sanctity of the American Dream is now undergoing arguably radical, even heretical, change. Across the US, states are rethinking the primacy of single-family zoning, which makes it possible to build multifamily housing in residential neighborhoods—with or without stealth, gentle, or disguised density. Oregon passed legislation eliminating exclusive single-family zoning in 2019. California followed in 2021 with SB 9: The California Home Act, which allows for up to four units on a single-family parcel and promotes infill development.[8] Its passage was not free from pushback. Under SB 9, landmarked and historic districts are exempt, so the City of Pasadena, a place known for both beautiful craftsman homes and racist histories of redlining, proposed an urgency ordinance declaring the entire city a landmark district, a move that garnered critical media attention and a warning by California Attorney General Rob Bonta.[9]

8   "Senate Bill 9 Is the Product of a Multi-Year Effort to Develop Solutions to Address California's Housing Crisis," https://focus.senate.ca.gov/sb9.
9   "Attorney General Bonta Puts City of Pasadena on Notice for Violating State Housing Laws," https://oag.ca.gov/news/press-releases/attorney-general-bonta-puts-city-pasadena-notice-violating-state-housing-laws.

The Outpost, a four-story, 16-unit project in Portland, Oregon, takes advantage of the state's higher-density policy and sets a new paradigm for both preservation and how we live together. Beebe Skidmore Architects preserved an existing nineteenth-century home on the property and worked with real estate developer Owen Gabbert and co-living platform Open Door to build a mini-tower: two handsome board-and-batten-clad cubes stacked with a twist.

From the outside, The Outpost's density doesn't appear particularly disguised. Its contemporary design displays few tropes of contextual sensitivity, like pitched roofs or vernacular overhangs, even though the other house on the site has both. What is concealed, however, is an experiment in communal living. Shared spaces include the kitchen plus dining and living areas. The project also offers a greater lesson, as disguised density asks us to question the sanctity of the single-family home. As reported by Jay Caspian Kang, suburban neighborhoods are more diverse than our collective imaginary.[10] Existing homes contain multiple generations, older single people, or groups of TikTok influencers. Designing multifamily housing within single-family neighborhoods challenges the notion of the nuclear family as the default resident.

10   "Everything You Think You Know About the Suburbs Is Wrong," https://www.nytimes.com/2021/11/18/opinion/suburbs-poor-diverse.html.

Designing with disguised density strategies allows housing to respond to shifting social and urban planning realities. But is it enough? Well-designed, dense, "missing-middle" housing is necessary to address scarcity and affordability; our language shouldn't hide the urgency. Disguised density may yield too much agency to NIMBY anxieties and, in doing so, favors modesty over the true need for larger, multiunit buildings.

Disguised Density Projects

Typical Floor Plans

■ Dwelling Unit

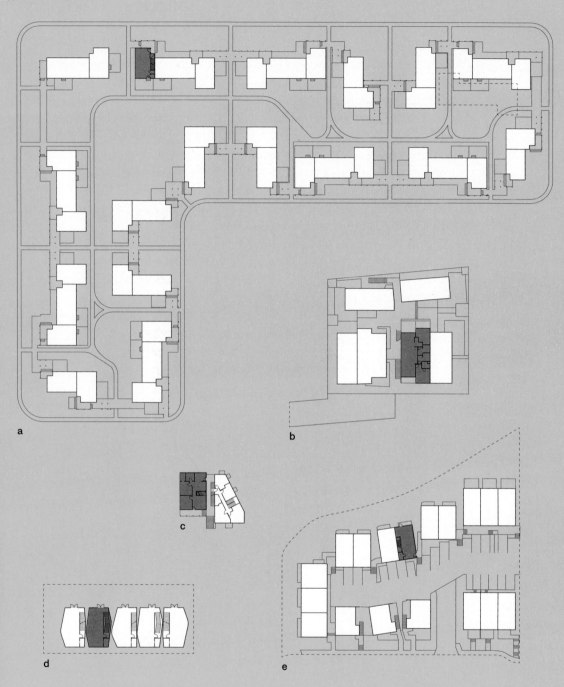

a   The Reserves at Gray Park, Duvall Decker, Greenville, MS
b   Ashland Apartments, Koning Eizenberg Architects, Santa Monica, CA
c   The Outpost, Beebe Skidmore Architects, Portland, OR
d   Canyon Drive, LOHA, Los Angeles, CA
e   Blackbirds, Bestor Architecture, Los Angeles, CA

Massive Murals

Whether to reinforce community identity or simply comply with municipal requirements, including local artists' work on the exterior facades or interior walls of multifamily housing has historically been implemented as an afterthought, but today it is taking center stage. Because the inclusion of one-off works can add exclusivity to bespoke interiors, murals are prone to accusations of artwashing. But when done well, commissioned murals can provide clear co-benefits: confronting the flat, uninviting face of an efficient cellular structure, murals can help transition the scale of a building to the human level. Inside, repetitive blank walls hiding services or circulation can benefit from artwork that improves corridors without sacrificing cost or units. In the case of Gravity, by NBBJ, oblique, short street walls are covered in a tessellated rainbow, overlaying artist Eduardo Kobra's monumental self-portrait. In ODA's Denizen project, single-loaded corridors sport multistory works of bright, abstracted creatures by The Bushwick Collective that are visible to the surrounding neighborhood through large windows. At the Gardner House and Allen Family Center in Seattle, by Runberg Architecture Group, twin plates of vivid painted flowers soften the asphalt of an urban lot abutting light rail.

Sketch Perspective Vignettes

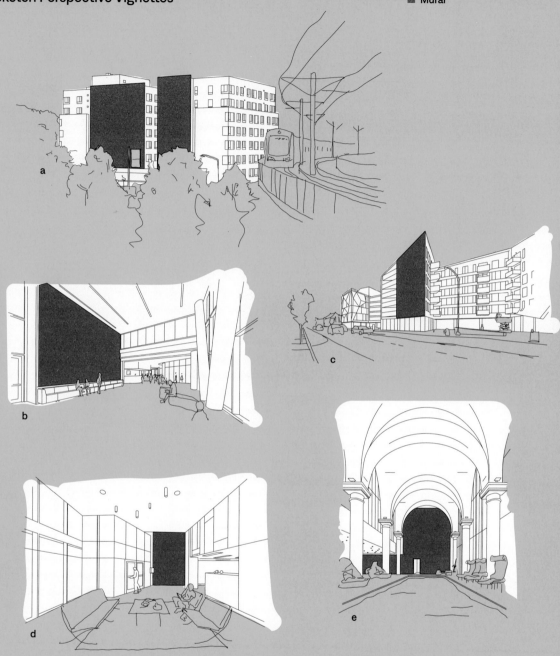

a   Gardner House and Allen Family Center, Runberg Architecture Group, Seattle, WA
    "White Ashes 10" by Kenji Hamai Stoll
b   Northtown Library and Apartments, Perkins&Will, Chicago, IL
    "Eclectic Current" by Chris Silva
c   Gravity, NBBJ, Columbus, OH
    Self-portrait by Eduardo Kobra
d   MLK Plaza, Magnusson Architecture and Planning, Bronx, NY
    Portrait of Martin Luther King Jr. by Tats Cru
e   Denizen, ODA, Brooklyn, NY
    "The Bushwick Collective" by Pixel Poncho and Aaron Li-Hill Interior

Three, Four, or Five over One, Sometimes Two

One architectural typology that featured heavily in our survey results was mid-rise podium housing. This is commonly known as five-over-one construction, which combines several inexpensive levels of light-wood framing above one level (sometimes two) of noncombustible concrete or steel construction (the moniker numbers also refer to the degree of fire resistance[i]). Building codes[ii] and zoning regulations often favor five-over-one buildings, which find the developmental sweet spot of density without pushing into high-rise categories and maximize the window-to-wall ratio in a compact volume. On the other hand, designers[iii] criticize them for being boxy and rigid and allowing for little variety in scale or modulation. Despite the parameters and critiques, many architects have embraced the form. In Minneapolis, Snow Kreilich Architects has wrapped a street corner in a sleek, dark volume of punched balconies and flush windows. The building's facade embraces its length and presence through a concise rhythm of apertures, with the ground floor receding in transparency. In Boise, Idaho, Pivot North Architects has stretched the type vertically, extending the podium over two levels and following a similar narrative of light cladding above a darker, shinier base. In Los Angeles, Kevin Daly Architects' Gramercy Senior Housing project flips the emphasis of depth to its primary-unit windows. The consistent internal logic of these projects highlights small variations in cladding and opening strategies, including window proportions shifting to optimize sunlight, cost, and rhythm. In all, they own the inherent structural logic to arrive at a vernacular that feels true to form and function. Indeed, there is virtue in this banality, and, according to the writer Alain de Botton, "architecture should have the confidence and kindness to be a little boring."

i See Table 601 ("Fire-Resistance Rating Requirements for Building Elements [Hours]") in the International Building Code, https://codes.iccsafe.org/content/IBC2015/chapter-6-types-of-construction.

ii Wood construction, being of a material more susceptible to combustion and disaster, is limited in height. Thus, it is placed on a pedestal of noncombustible construction to gain the maximum amount of floor space within local zoning limits and before the building is categorized as a "high-rise."

iii "Why Do All New Apartment Buildings Look the Same?" https://archive.curbed.com/2018/12/4/18125536/real-estate-modern-apartment-architecture.

■ Combustable Construction

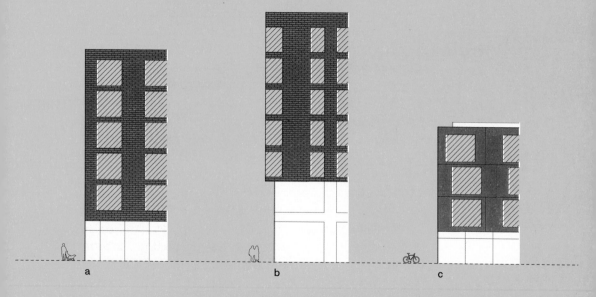

a
b
c

a   Second + Second, Snow Kreilich Architects, Minneapolis, MN
b   Thomas Logan, Pivot North Architects, Boise, ID
c   Gramercy Senior Housing, Kevin Daly Architects, Los Angeles, CA

Working with Water

Climate change is exacerbating both extreme flood and drought events. In recent years, this has pressured housing design to accommodate planting strategies, conserve water, and instill overall resiliency. Alongside energy and carbon reduction targets, water has been a defining lens through which we see projects both performing as infrastructure and creating a captivating environment. Inside the building, greywater capture, tankless systems, closed-circuit piping, an absence of roof drains, and low-flow fixtures are increasingly the norm—resulting in slimmer, more recycled hydrological systems. Outside the building envelope, absorbent landscapes form swales, basins, and berms that display collection and containment. Large-scale projects contend with tidal shifts and compensatory storage requirements, often resulting in a change in ground-floor uses and site strategies. Cities such as New York, Boston, and San Francisco continue to develop sea-level rise resilience strategies, while their waterfronts only become denser as housing needs grow. Projects in municipalities known for rainy climates, such as Portland and Seattle, have been quick to embrace the experiential and physical benefits of working with water. In parallel, groundwater infiltration zones in the Southwest result in much more xeriscaped and drought-tolerant projects. Resultant designs are often softer and use native flora. In diverse ways, water capture, mitigation, and retention are surgically used as tools to make housing more resilient in the face of an increasingly unpredictable climate.

As climate pressures continue, design can shape how we address relationships between both outside and inside, wet and dry—as well as their associated maintenance protocols. New guidelines, such as WEDG (Waterfront Edge Design Guidelines), expand upon the model of other certification agencies (such as LEED or PHIUS) to provide useful baseline assumptions across geographies. After Hurricane Harvey in 2017, the American Institute of Architects (AIA) Houston similarly turned its attention to resiliency, forming the AIA Disaster Resilience Task Force[i] and releasing a brief homeowner's guide to rebuilding for resilience that outlines direct material and assembly suggestions.[ii] Houston and Tampa released resiliency plans in 2020 and 2021, respectively. At the opposite extreme, design deals with drought by offering methods to conserve and operate without regular levels of water use. In 2022, Las Vegas banned grass lawns in an effort to reduce water use in residential areas. In his essay, Timothy Schuler delves into notable projects that tackle these challenges and explores how their designs mediate both experiential and infrastructural relationships to water.

i   "Disaster Assistance Program: A Nationwide Network of Architects to Help Communities Before and After a Disaster," https://www.aia.org/resources/69766-disaster-assistance-program.
ii "Resiliency," https://aiahouston.org/v/resiliency/.

by Timothy Schuler

In 2022, for the first time in the country's history, the US government declared a Tier 2 shortage for the Colorado River, triggering massive cuts to the water allotments of states such as Arizona and Nevada, and in some places reducing users' available water by nearly half. It marked an intensification of the already-historic Tier 1 restrictions, announced by the Department of the Interior in August 2021, the same month Hurricane Ida devastated portions of the Gulf Coast and brought unprecedented flooding to the Mid-Atlantic. The storm—the worst hurricane to hit Louisiana since Katrina—killed 87 people.

Such extremes—megadroughts in one part of the country, historic flooding in another—are, according to scientists, a reality of global climate change and likely constitute a new normal for the US.

Though it tends to get less attention than energy-efficiency or financing strategies, water intersects with housing design in a variety of ways. First, flooding remains the country's most frequent and most expensive disaster,[1] costing an average of $32 billion each year, a figure that could reach $41 billion by 2050. Flood risk is not distributed equally. Formerly redlined neighborhoods, for instance, which often remain more accessible to renters and first-time homebuyers and are therefore more diverse, tend to have larger concentrations of homes at high risk of flooding than historically greenlined areas. In Sacramento, 21.6 percent of homes in historically redlined or yellowlined neighborhoods face severe flood risk, compared with just 11.8 percent of homes in more desirable areas.

[1] "Flooding: Our Nation's Most Frequent and Costly Natural Disaster," https://www.fbiic.gov /public/2010/mar/Flooding HistoryandCausesFS.pdf.

The country's disaster recovery infrastructure is equally inequitable. In the wake of a flood or other disaster, Black Americans routinely receive fewer aid dollars than white Americans. According to the Center for American Progress, on average, the wealth of a Black disaster victim decreases by approximately $27,000, while the wealth of a white victim increases by approximately $126,000. This is due to several factors, including the fact that Black Americans are more likely to be renters, tend to receive lower appraisals on the value of their homes when they do own their homes, and pay higher insurance premiums, leading a portion of owners in low-lying areas not to carry flood insurance at all.

[2] "Rio Verde Homeowners Hit Hard by City Water Shut-Off," https://www.scottsdale.org /city_news/rio-verde -homez4a-9068-11ed-9de8 -afe898f219b1.html.

In the West, meanwhile, water scarcity increasingly determines how and where new housing is built, as utilities place moratoria on new water hookups or, in the case of Rio Verde Foothills, Arizona, municipalities cease water delivery to new developments after construction is complete.[2]

Of course, the relationship is reciprocal. How and where the nation builds new housing impacts nearby water resources

Though undetectable in its outdoor spaces, Silver Star Apartments has an onsite treatment system consisting of textile filters, microfiltration, and disinfection.

The 49-unit Silver Star Apartments is made up of three buildings around a central courtyard.

and increases the pressure on urban stormwater systems. Continued urbanization, combined with aging infrastructure and more severe storms, means that heavy rain events are capable of maxing out cities' stormwater systems. In cities with combined sewer and stormwater infrastructure, this can lead to harmful overflows, in which untreated sewage enters local waterways, posing threats to both local ecosystems and public health.

In response to these and other challenges, housing projects around the country are piloting ever-more-sophisticated approaches to onsite water reuse and retention, delivering housing that is climate-resilient and community-oriented. Often, these advances are being driven by municipal stormwater codes, which are being updated in response to growing environmental concerns, as well as federal consent decrees under the Clean Water Act. Once hidden below ground in pipes, this water infrastructure is increasingly celebrated, doubling as an amenity, habitat, or part of the building's basic form.

At Silver Star Apartments in Los Angeles, a 49-unit affordable housing development for formerly unhoused veterans completed in 2020, FSY Architects worked with Yael Lir Landscape Architects and Biohabitats to design a greywater treatment system that meets 100 percent of the demand for non-potable water. The system saves 480,000 gallons of water per year and reduces potable water consumption by 25 percent.

At Othello Gardens, an 11-unit townhouse development on the south side of Seattle, Wittman Estes integrated the necessary bioretention into the very architecture of the buildings, designing a system of vertically stacked, cascading planters that reduce the amount, flow rate, and pollutant load of associated rainwater runoff. Still other projects, such as Tillamook Row in Portland, Oregon, feature aboveground cisterns sized to be part of a community-scale, disaster-resilience infrastructure, storing enough water to serve members of the surrounding community in the event of a utility-crippling seismic event.

These and other projects demonstrate that new housing, even if not built in flood-prone areas, can help conserve water resources and decrease the risk of flooding by easing the burden on cities' stormwater systems. Well-designed housing can increase a community's overall resilience and become a type of collective, public infrastructure whose benefits radiate outward, well beyond the sphere of the individual occupant. This is a view of housing that treats the home not only as a private asset, but also as part of a commons that can contribute to the safety and well-being of an entire community.

Unlike the underlying causes of the country's spiking housing costs, the challenges posed by water vary widely by region. In arid places, available

The four stories of the Othello Gardens townhomes allow for rainwater to filter at numerous points as it cascades down through a series of bio-filtration planters. Pervious paving and Grasscrete contribute to water filtration.

water resources constrain the design and construction of new housing, both at the development scale and at the building scale. In wetter regions, designers are increasingly mandated to manage stormwater runoff on-site, impacting the size, layout, and number of units that can be built, as well as form, materiality, and circulation. As the country saw with a catastrophic atmospheric river event in California in early 2023, many regions are increasingly grappling with both extremes: long periods of extreme heat and drought, punctuated by overwhelming precipitation.

Some cities have even begun to use additional density—in the form of either FAR (floor area ratio) or building height—as an incentive to coax developers to build green stormwater infrastructure. For Verso, a 173-unit market-rate housing development in Beaverton, Oregon, a suburb of Portland, Ankrom Moisan exploited a provision in the zoning code that permitted additional height if enough stormwater could be managed onsite and in a way that served as a neighborhood amenity. To satisfy the requirement, the design team, which included AKS Engineering & Forestry, pulled one corner of the building back, creating enough space for a wedge-shaped, boulder-strewn rain garden that manages all the rainwater runoff from the roof.

Challenges associated with water vary not only from region to region but from site to site. At Tillamook Row, a pocket row-house community in Portland's Eliot neighborhood, stormwater infiltration was impossible due to the site's high-clay soils. "If you dig a hole on that site, and you pour water into it, you have a pool," says Stephen Aiguier, the founder and president of Green Hammer, which designed the project for BCMC Properties. Typically, the firm deploys dry wells or bioswales to manage stormwater, but here Green Hammer and Medium Landscape Architecture had to resort to a pair of lined retention ponds—one at the east end of the central lawn and a smaller one along the street.

The ponds are filled with water-loving plant species and boulders to absorb or reduce the flow rate of rainwater runoff. Any water that falls on the row houses' metal roofs or the ground plane flows into one of the two ponds. (The water for the aforementioned aboveground cisterns is collected after being filtered through a series of vegetated roofs.) What doesn't evaporate or get used by the plants overflows into the city's stormwater system—something Aiguier, who lived at Tillamook Row for several years, rarely saw happen. "What I noticed is that the retention pond can handle a tremendous amount of water," he says. "It was pretty rare that it was actually overflowing."

For Station House, a 110-unit affordable housing development in Seattle's Capitol Hill neighborhood, the architects at Schemata Workshop also faced site conditions that precluded any sort of stormwater infiltration, in this

Timothy Schuler

A large rain garden at Verso captures rainwater from the roof and provides a natural streetscape for residents and neighbors alike.

case because the development sat directly atop a Sound Transit light-rail station. "We didn't want water to get into the ground and start leaching into the tunnel—or worse, causing more pressure on the tunnel itself," explains Grace Kim, cofounder of Schemata Workshop, which designed the project with Seattle's Berger Partnership. A series of extensive green roofs and a rooftop garden capture rainwater that falls on the roof, while a long, curvilinear bioswale takes runoff from a central plaza, minimizing how much stormwater enters the city's system.

Though marketed mainly as an amenity, the steel planters that comprise the rooftop garden play a significant role in managing water. Whereas the typical sedum-planted extensive green roof has, perhaps, six inches of soil, raised planters can hold up to 24 inches of soil. During rain events, those planters become sponges. "More soil is more water capacity," Kim says.

Compared with other water-retention strategies, the planters also offer a host of co-benefits, from providing habitat for birds and insects to allowing residents to grow their own food. "We were trying to be smart about how we caught and retained water," Kim says. "We didn't want to create a big cistern in the basement of the building, both from a weight standpoint and also because land is precious. We would rather spend the money and space to house people than to store water."

Seven miles south of Station House, in Seattle's Othello neighborhood, Othello Gardens also uses rooftop planters as part of its stormwater management approach. Rather than being conveyed directly into ground-level planters, however, excess water is directed to downspouts that channel the water to three consecutive levels of bioretention planters. The planters, which together hold 615 cubic feet of soil, are integrated into a series of stepped balconies and alcoves, punctuating the townhomes' brick facades with bursts of greenery. (The specific placement and configuration of the planters depends on the building's orientation.)

Each planter is essentially a bathtub, explains Matt Wittman, a principal and cofounder of Wittman Estes. When the uppermost planter fills up, the water flows into the planter directly below it, and so on. This creates an invisible cascade that, in its final iteration, manages more than 172,000 gallons of stormwater per year, exceeding the requirements of the city's stormwater code.

Those requirements were one of two main drivers for the project's vertical bioretention system, Wittman says: "The city has fairly robust requirements for stormwater management with these bioretention planters," and it's challenging to find sufficient space, particularly on housing projects in dense, urban neighborhoods. "We thought, what if you just put the bioretention planters on the building itself? Basically you're

Timothy Schuler

Tillamook Row's central courtyard hosts the above-ground water cistern; the project's onsite rainwater system can hold up to 3,600 gallons of water.

taking an infrastructure that's usually deployed horizontally and stacking it vertically onto the building."

The other main driver was the history of the site, an old farmstead where Ted Peterson, the developer, grew up. Peterson had memories of Rainier Valley when it was mostly orchards and cattle ranches, and he wanted the project to evoke pieces of that history. "That was kind of the design brief," Wittman says. "How do you make housing with this high density and still express this idea of gardens? So, thinking of water like they would have as farmers was fundamental." The prominence of the planters contributes to this sense of history and identity, as does the materiality of the ground-level pedestrian and parking areas, where "paths" of permeable Grasscrete lead to building entrances, a visual clue to the project's sensitivity to water that doubles as wayfinding.

Novel systems require especially close coordination during construction, however. At Othello Gardens, the pipes connecting the exterior planters run partially inside the exterior wall, which necessitated additional detailing and a meticulous eye toward waterproofing. "You're effectively building pools on the building," Wittman explains. "You have to be really good about doing the proper detailing, both structurally, because there's a weight component with the saturated soil, and then with the plumbing, because you have daisy chains of plumbing and overflows, where water drains out into an overflow, and that overflow is captured in a pipe that then goes into the building, and then comes back out again. So, you definitely have to have a good contractor." In the case of Othello Gardens, Wittman says there was an understanding between the contractor and the subs that the bioretention planters, drainage, and building envelope were "part of an integrated whole."

Even as architects, designers, engineers, and landscape architects find ever-more creative ways to slow, capture, and reuse water, high barriers remain. Chief among them is the upfront cost of systems. Unlike, say, solar photovoltaic systems, water-conservation strategies, such as greywater treatment systems, struggle to pay for themselves over time, partially because the cost savings associated with them are relatively low, but also because some water utilities charge higher rates the less water a household uses. In Portland, Oregon, for instance, "if you use less water, your fees go up," Aiguier says. "That's to make up for this infrastructure problem."

At the same time, the public sector is driving much of the innovation in site-scale stormwater management through updates to local codes. This, in turn, is beginning to shape the feel and functionality of the built environment. Jody Estes, a landscape architect and cofounder of Wittman Estes, says more designers need to embrace regulations and building codes as a way to find new formal expression, as her firm did at Othello Gardens. "I think a lot of architects see the bio-retention requirement here as a problem," she says. "Don't see it as a problem. See it as a great opportunity."

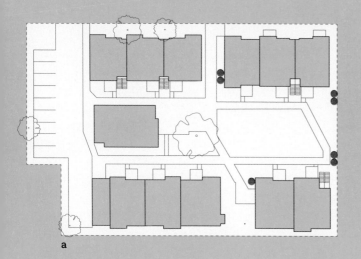

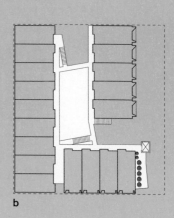

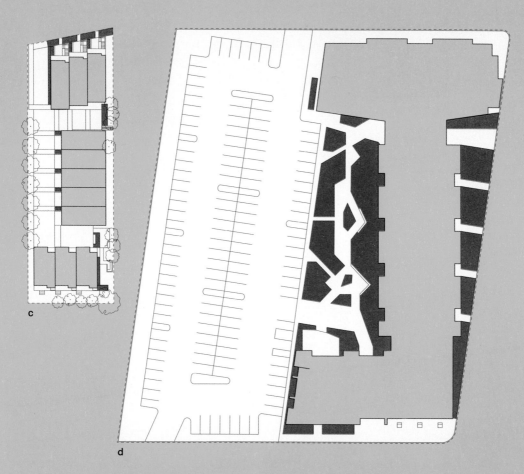

a   Tillamook Row, Green Hammer, Portland, OR
b   Silver Star Apartments, FSY Architects, Los Angeles, CA
c   Othello Gardens, Wittman Estes, Seattle, WA
d   Verso, Ankrom Moisan, Beaverton, OR

Accessory and Additional Units

Accessory dwelling units (ADUs)[i]—small, second dwellings sited on the same lot as a primary single-family home[ii]—have recently gained new political, media, and architectural attention. It's not hard to see why: because ADUs can add density without drastically changing existing neighborhood character, they have proved effective at expanding the imagination around the typical single-home lot. At the low-profile extreme, Co-Housing Denver, by design firm Productora, includes ADUs that simply operate as an extension of the primary structure and are visually similar in hierarchy and materiality. On the opposite end is The Block Project in Seattle, which features ADUs permitted, built, and operated by an outside organization for people experiencing homelessness. Here, the lot owner essentially leases the land (*gratis*, in this case) for the construction of a clearly differentiated structure. Taking a similar approach, the OBY House model, designed by CoEverything and run by OBY Collective, pays homeowners to install carbon-neutral units. Although ADUs don't represent a perfect solution to the affordability crisis, their pragmatic, incremental nature opens the single-family lot to density and experimentation with alternative possibilities of both form and ownership.

i   ADUs are also referred to as granny flats, garage apartments, or even further subdivisions of an existing dwelling structure. They can be a basement flat or a new detached volume in the backyard. Recently, especially in less dense, single-family neighborhoods, policy shifts have rezoned for their approval as a way to densify with little disruption of the existing residential fabric.

ii   Although ADUs are often implemented through overlay zoning or pilot programs, they relate heavily to the movement to eliminate single-family zoning altogether. In 2019, Minneapolis became the first major city to ban single-family zoning. The same year, Oregon passed a similar law statewide. In 2022, California followed suit, banning single-family zoning across the state.

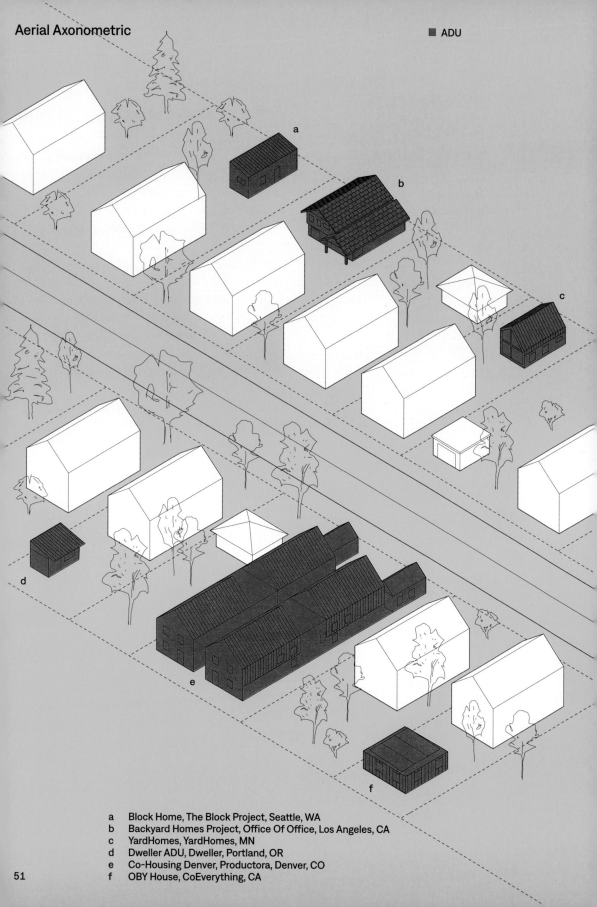

■ ADU

a Block Home, The Block Project, Seattle, WA
b Backyard Homes Project, Office Of Office, Los Angeles, CA
c YardHomes, YardHomes, MN
d Dweller ADU, Dweller, Portland, OR
e Co-Housing Denver, Productora, Denver, CO
f OBY House, CoEverything, CA

Pitching Roofs

Whether evoking a local vernacular or reconfiguring an age-old domestic motif,[i] contemporary architects seem to abide by one rule when pitching roofs over multifamily dwellings: uneven gables are king. At both the townhome and mid-rise scale, projects are experimenting with increased slope to celebrate water-shedding properties and create a more dramatic roofline silhouette. At The Clara, by Holst Architecture in Eagle, Idaho, exaggerating the overhang lends dramatic flair and drops deep shadows to vary the regular facades. In Pittsfield, Massachusetts, Utile employed subtly different angles on the roof of the Tyler Street Development to create an effect of movement when taken as a whole. At Bastion Community Housing, by OJT, shotgun-esque duplex units are defined by their asymmetric roofs, which cantilever over their covered entry ramps and terminate without turning the corner. In Vancouver, Access Architecture subtly sloped several volumes of a three-story walk-up housing block. Alternating eaves are flush with the facade and often cut off when recessed balconies or common spaces are expressed. Across projects, the roofs resist overhanging, prioritizing volume over planes. These uneven gables impress an attitude of timid familiarity with contextual constraints while simultaneously being novel—blending housing's demand for anonymity and real estate's demand for allure.

i   Pitched roofs or gabled roofs come in many shapes. Typically, they are symmetrical and overhang on the sides for structure and style, and their pitch responds to climate demands to shed frozen or liquid water in the most efficient manner possible.

Cropped Roof Elevations

∠ Approximate Roof Angle

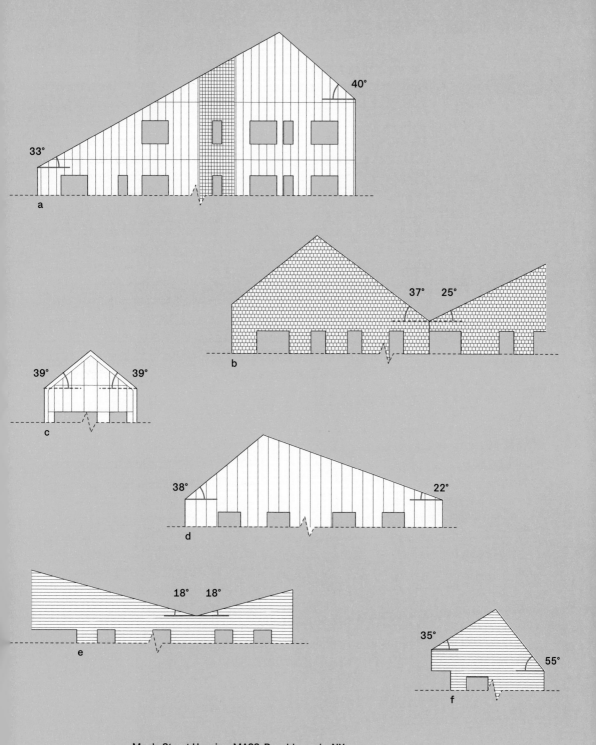

a   Maple Street Housing, MASS, Poughkeepsie, NY
b   The Clara, Holst Architecture, Eagle, ID
c   Cornerstone Apartments, MMW Architecture, Missoula, MT
d   Pittsfield Tyler Street Development, Utile, Pittsfield, MA
e   The Elwood, Access Architecture, Vancouver, WA
f   Bastion Community Housing, OJT, New Orleans, LA

The New Era of Amenity

With increasing pressure on the public sector to employ all measures to expand the supply of affordable housing, municipalities are looking to leverage more value out of underused public land—which has led to new and interesting developments that mix housing with typically standalone public service buildings. One aspect of this strategy is co-location, which conceptually pairs programs that work for a specific resident group (such as seniors) and a chosen public amenity (such as after-school care). By coupling social infrastructure with housing, these projects expand the typological imagination for public land beyond other housing proposals that use air rights or remediation strategies to capture value. The best projects push pairings of residences and amenities beyond mere adjacency and into an active partnership. Programming thus enriches the housing experience while providing invaluable social infrastructure to communities that may be under-resourced. Architecturally, this method has also been shown to give new life to the current standard of podium building in the US, replacing traditional retail programs at the ground floor (which are struggling nationally) with community resources, such as child care, learning centers, and job training. Projects investing in co-location or service-oriented amenities have incorporated thoughtful design approaches to these constraints to both give more value to a single site and expand what housing as a social service can—and should—accomplish.

We found that using these strategies simultaneously increases urban heterogeneity and resident benefits. Projects' exterior and interior expressions often heighten the contrast of uses for heroic effect rather than treating the housing as background, or the civic spaces as simply infrastructure. As a path forward for many publicly owned sites, these projects also exhibit a much greater possibility for a vibrant urban metabolism than typical isolated and one-note housing projects. Projecting forward, amenities and co-location strategies built into the framework of multifamily developments may become a necessary design factor in shaping fully resourced and interconnected communities. In his essay, Nate Berg traces the development and resident experiences of several co-located housing schemes in Chicago; Seattle; Columbus, Ohio; Santa Fe, New Mexico; and New York.

by Nate Berg

Chicago's public library system had a vision. It was the mid-2010s, and many libraries had been built across the city in recent years. They were modestly designed cookie-cutter branch locations that made up for what they lacked in size and resources by being located within walking distance of most of the city's residents. The Chicago Public Library (CPL) wanted to build off this momentum. Former CPL Commissioner Andrea Telli says the system envisioned creating the twenty-first-century library, a multifunctional institution that would have a much broader mission than lending books. This new kind of library would support economic development, nurture learning, engender or support community, and provide social services needed in the area. The vision was grand. But what CPL didn't have was the budget to pull it off.

In late 2016, then-Mayor Rahm Emanuel proposed a unique solution. CPL would be able to realize its twenty-first-century library by joining forces with partners who could access the funding to get stuff built: housing developers. By coupling new projects—federally subsidized affordable apartment buildings with libraries co-located on the same site or even within the same building—the city could get more housing, and the library system could get more of the ambitious libraries it envisioned. And by giving communities the well-designed library branches residents already wanted, the city was more easily able to garner support for affordable housing projects that neighbors often oppose.

A design competition was launched, and some of the city's most notable architects pitched ideas. Less than three years later, three of these housing-library combinations were opened, creating a total of 161 new apartments for seniors, Chicago Housing Authority residents, and some market-rate renters. The most striking of these projects is the Independence branch and apartments in Chicago's Irving Park neighborhood. With 44 subsidized affordable apartments available specifically to seniors, a light-filled two-story library, and a shared courtyard in the back, Independence is the model of the twenty-first-century library CPL had envisioned. "If you're trying to strengthen community and community engagement, it's a wonderful concept to have senior apartments above a library building," says Telli.

This approach of fusing community amenities and housing is catching on. Independence and the two other housing-library combinations in Chicago are just a few of the growing number of housing projects being built with community-forming spaces, social services, or the leisurely "third places" people crave outside their homes and jobs.

Many, but not all, of these projects are affordable housing developments, and this method of building homes alongside a diverse array of amenities is being used across the country. In the Bronx, the Peninsula is a mixed-use project that combines affordable apartments, incubation space for food-related startups, and a community-serving grocery store into a cluster of contemporary mid-rise buildings.[1] Columbus, Ohio, has Gravity,[2] a multipronged housing community encompassing mindfulness, mental health, and wellness providers, with modern residences, offices, and retail spaces built around the kinds of common areas that might host a movie night or a food truck. In Santa Fe, Siler Yard is an affordable live/work development for artists in low-rise apartments and townhomes oriented around a plaza.[3] And in Seattle, Gardner House and the Allen Family Center is a multitextured housing complex built to accommodate the unique needs of families who have experienced homelessness.[4]

These projects are broadening the concept of mixed-use development—the archetypal housing above ground-floor retail—with a more deliberate pairing of the kinds of services, resources, and amenities residents want and need. A new genre of multifunctional, social-leaning projects is rewriting the housing playbook. With innovative designs backed by mold-breaking financing, these projects are creating new pathways for multifunctional and community-forging projects, at both affordable and market rates. They're showing that housing can be redesigned to do much more than put a roof over someone's head.

In a country where building affordable housing has gradually fallen to the fringes of civic responsibility, the method of binding affordable residential development with community-serving amenities has found surprising currency.

Not every co-located housing project is affordable by nature, but many are mission-driven in one form or another. In Seattle, Gardner House and the Allen Family Center is a standout example of a do-good project. It's an attractive eight-story building with 95 apartments, an interior courtyard and playground that look out over the street, and a community room and kitchen for events. Developed as a public-private partnership between the City of Seattle and the national nonprofit developer Mercy Housing's Northwest regional office,[5] with a critical $30 million funding grant from the Paul G. Allen Family Foundation and $5 million from the city, the project was designed with a particular community in mind. The apartments are set aside for families that have recently experienced homelessness, and a significant amount of ground-floor square footage houses a novel community resource center targeting those at risk of or experiencing homelessness. The resource center concentrates

1   The Peninsula Mixed-Use Campus, https://www.wxystudio.com/projects/architecture/spofford_mixeduse_redevelopment.
2   "Wellness Centers Are the New Golf Course Retirement Community," https://www.fastcompany.com/90686911/wellness-centers-are-the-new-golf-course-retirement-community.
3   "In a City Besieged by Rent Hikes, Santa Fe Scores an Affordable Housing Complex for Artists," https://southwestcontemporary.com/in-a-city-besieged-by-rent-hikes-santa-fe-scores-an-affordable-housing-complex-for-artists/.
4   "Gardner House and Allen Family Center," https://www.mercyhousing.org/northwest/allen-family-center-faq/.
5   "Mercy Housing Northwest," https://www.mercyhousing.org/northwest/.

The affordable housing units at Independence Library and Apartments feature large windows and balconies highlighted by bright colors.

Public spaces at the Peninsula invite leisure and gathering.

Large open spaces at Gravity In Columbus, Ohio, provide residents ample room to move together.

The New Era of Amenity

the multiple government and support agencies used by these populations, making it easier for a family to access help from various social services that are rarely coordinated with each other and often located in disparate places. "We created a one-stop shop for all these different resources," says Colin Morgan-Cross, director of real estate for Mercy Housing Northwest.

Located on a trapezoidal lot, the building has a welcoming plaza on one end, and its yellow-accented windows present a sunny face toward the light-rail that runs directly alongside. The 8,000-square-foot community resource center, also carrying yellow accents on its facade, takes up the entire ground floor of the building. It's an unusually large amount of space for a project to devote to social services, which are typically shunted into tiny corners on the rare occasions that developers include them in their plans. For Mercy Housing, though, it's a somewhat common commitment. The organization was founded by a group of nuns in Omaha in 1981, and community-serving amenities are included in many of its developments. Morgan-Cross says the organization works with its projects' architects to find ways to create community-serving spaces by repurposing parts of the floorplan that are less than ideal for residential units, particularly those on the ground floor. Gardner House, designed by Seattle-based Runberg Architecture Group,[6] sits at the corner of two busy arterial streets and near multiple transit lines, so street-facing ground-floor spaces with minimal residential appeal became the Allen Family Center. "It wasn't about giving up another use," Morgan-Cross says. "It was about meeting a need."

6   Runberg Architecture Group, https://runberg.com/.

The services provided on site are varied and are intended both for residents and for members of the community at large. The center offers homelessness prevention and housing placement, financial stability and job training, mental and behavioral health treatment, and naturalization and legal services oriented toward immigrants and refugees.

This may sound like the altruistic, bleeding-heart work of an organization founded by nuns, but Morgan-Cross says dedicating space to these services makes sense for the residents and Mercy Housing alike. Resident services staff are employed by the project, serving almost like housing-focused social workers. They help residents keep on track with rent and utility payments and operate an eviction prevention program to help residents keep their apartments while reducing turnover for Mercy Housing Northwest.

The concentration of services at Gardner House serves several purposes, not least of which is satisfying the needs of the specific community of residents living there. Morgan-Cross says Mercy Housing's projects will continue to include these kinds of services and amenities going forward but probably not at this scale. The concept is replicable, in theory, he says. "I just wish it was also replicable to get major philanthropic grants every time we needed them."

The Allen Family Center's entrance is off a mini corner plaza on the bottom floor of the Gardner House. Various building cutouts and terraces connect the building's programs to each other and to the surrounding context.

In Chicago, the library-housing combination projects were realized largely because they were pet projects of the city's powerful mayor. When the design competition launched in late 2016, the architects and developers competing separately for the projects could be confident they'd get built. As one of few cities with its own allocation of coveted 9 percent federal Low-Income Housing Tax Credits,[7] which end up covering about 70 percent of project costs, Chicago had valuable tools at its disposal. As mayor, Emanuel had significant sway in determining which projects received those 9 percent tax credits, as well as other city and state housing funds.

7   "An Overview of the Low-Income Housing Tax Credit (LIHTC)," https://taxfoundation.org/low-income-housing-tax-credit-lihtc/.

The mayoral support and ambitious programming attracted the city's leading lights of design, including Skidmore, Owings & Merrill and Perkins&Will. In total, 32 firms competed for the three library-housing combination projects the city was pursuing.

For the Independence branch, the city's evaluation committee selected a design by Chicago-based John Ronan Architects,[8] which stacked and segmented the two parts of the six-story building. The concrete-and-glass library is pulled up to the property line on a busy street, and the bright-gray four-story apartment block for low-income seniors sits farther back. Colorfully accented windows pop out from the apartment's corrugated metal facade, and full-height windows line both lengths of the library, pouring natural light into a reading room with an impressive 40-foot-high ceiling. "I want people walking into that library to feel important, and to feel this is an important institution," Ronan says.

8   John Ronan Architects, http://www.jrarch.com/independence-library-and-apartments-1.
9   "Independence Library and Apartments," https://www.aia.org/showcases/6292944-independence-library-and-apartments.
10   Evergreen Real Estate Group, https://www.evergreenreg.com/.

The 16,000-square-foot library and 44-unit apartment building cost a total of $33.4 million and bring an award-winning piece of contemporary architecture to Irving Park.[9] From the street, residents can look up to the multicolored balconies that pop out from the bright facade and point to their units. Color is used as a tool for both resident pride and neighborhood engagement. "One of the agendas of the project as I saw it was to change how people think about affordable housing and be more welcoming of it in their communities," Ronan says.

Ronan's firm was paired with Evergreen Real Estate Group,[10] which had been selected to develop two of the three library-housing projects based on a still-baking plan for financing them. The timeline called for projects to be under construction by 2018.

"While we had a lovely competition-winning design in March of 2017, we didn't have anything else," says David Block, director of development for Evergreen Real Estate Group. The site needed entitlements, community outreach had not yet begun, and there was no formal financing plan nor lender to make Evergreen's side of the funding available. "We had to do all that in essentially nine months."

The crunched timeline made for a challenging design and development process, but Ronan came with some relevant experience. His firm had previously designed a few high schools with public library branches on site. "It was kind of in our sweet spot," he says.

To ensure each component of the project had its own identity and didn't feel tacked on to the other, Ronan used contrasting facade treatments and staggered the volumes. At the rear of the building, the library's second floor juts outward to create a green terrace, which is intended for the residents but is also used occasionally by the library, forming a unique shared civic space. "Let's take advantage of these two types of buildings coming together and create a place where people can interact," Ronan says of that design move.

Co-location is only part of the recipe. For these two buildings to actually complement each other, Ronan says the project teams had to put extra effort into drafting guidelines for exactly how the two different audiences could use the space, and under what circumstances. "It's not enough to envision it and design it," he says. "You have to think through the policy aspect of it."

Block's company is currently in the process of developing two other housing-library combinations in Colorado and Massachusetts. They're signs that projects like these don't necessarily need a political bigwig as their champion nor an infusion of philanthropic largesse to take shape.

The federal tax credits used to develop the Chicago project require Block's company to hold the property for 15 years, but he expects to keep it in his portfolio for much longer. "The building is full and stays full because people like living there," Block says.

Wendy Jo Harmston was one of the project's first residents, and she has no plans to leave. A voracious reader, Harmston says she checks out three or four books a week from the library and uses its computers. She knows the staff there now, and residents in the building know she can usually be found downstairs in the reading room. "I rarely miss a day," she says.

A former community organizer who has lived in the area for years, Harmston was part of the chorus of neighbors calling for a library to be built on that site, where a previous library had burned down. Although not expecting to, she ended up needing the affordable rent the building's apartments provide. Like many of her fellow senior residents, the building is allowing her to age in a place she knows. And she's starting to know the people, too.

A community is gradually taking shape among the people who have found themselves living in this novel kind of building, one made especially for them. "We're all in a certain age group," Harmston says. "It's kind of neat that we're experiencing new things. Not just different, but new."

The New Era of Amenity Projects
Amenity Floor Plans

■ Amenity Space

a   Independence Library and Apartments, John Ronan Architects, Chicago, IL
b   The Peninsula Mixed-Use Campus, WXY Studio, Bronx, NY
c   Gardner House and Allen Family Center, Runberg Architecture Group, Seattle, WA

d   Gravity, NBBJ, Columbus, OH

To the Moon and Back (Yard)

3D printers—once a humble desktop technology used for making architectural models—have come a long way in recent years. Their ability to handle hardier materials has opened up enormous possibilities. Although early architecturally printed fabrications used clay, soil, and even spider silk, current 3D dwellings mostly rely on an extrusion of concrete[i] to form ribbed bearing walls that can be infilled with doors, windows, and roofs. One company, ICON, has captured media attention for its tiny home village outside of Austin, Texas,[ii] and its partnership with NASA,[iii] completing homes quickly, with vastly reduced human labor, and promising future developments on the moon. In Austin, Logan Architecture's East 17th St. Residences use ICON's construction method. The setup relies on a gantry-like rig over each plot, from which a moving nozzle extrudes layer upon layer of concrete—leaving room for openings—and circles back to where it started. Other companies, such as Alquist 3D, focus more locally (on planet Earth), creating homes for Habitat for Humanity and targeting rural areas as ideal candidates for quick and affordable (timber-free) housing. Another firm, Hannah, has designed what might be the country's first two-story, 3D-printed house.[iv] As the field stands, the carbon-intensive use of concrete through an energy-intensive, onsite fabrication process adds caveats to what is often marketed as a revolutionary ideal. Concrete curves around every corner—used as the water table, interior finish, and flashing—exhibit both the wide potential and limits of a material that, though applied in fluid techniques, remains as fixed as ever. Similarly, material and labor savings will depend on how the technology evolves beyond simply printing a structural frame. In contrast, the BioHome3D in Orono, Maine, developed and designed by the University of Maine and Oak Ridge National Laboratory, claims to be the world's first 3D-printed house made entirely with bio-based, recyclable materials. The walls, floors, and roof are printed with a combination of wood fibers and bio-resins. The exterior hardly gives form to the structure's fluid origins, presenting an alternative future to a technology that continues to expand in scale across the solar system.

i   However, at least one company is experimenting with printing wood products; see "3D Printing with Wood Products," https://umainetoday.umaine.edu/stories/2019/3d-printing-with-wood-products/.

ii   "ICON and Lennar Started 3D Printing a 100-Home Community," https://www.3dprintingmedia.network/icon-and-lennar-started-3d-printing-a-100-home-community/.

iii   "ICON to Develop Lunar Surface Construction System with $57.2 Million NASA Award," https://www.iconbuild.com/newsroom/icon-to-develop-lunar-surface-construction-system-with-57-2-million-nasa-award.

iv   "3D-Printed Homes Level Up with a 2-Story House in Houston," https://www.npr.org/2023/01/16/1148943607/3d-printed-homes-level-up-with-a-2-story-house-in-houston.

Axonometric Fragments

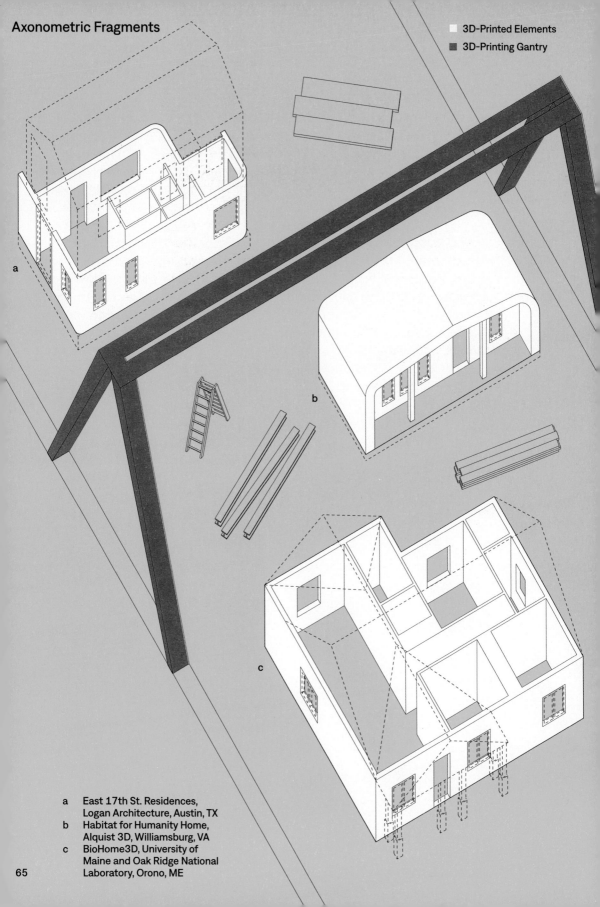

3D-Printed Elements

3D-Printing Gantry

a

b

c

a   East 17th St. Residences,
     Logan Architecture, Austin, TX

b   Habitat for Humanity Home,
     Alquist 3D, Williamsburg, VA

c   BioHome3D, University of
     Maine and Oak Ridge National
     Laboratory, Orono, ME

Color Blocking

As energy models increasingly push for a tighter window-to-wall ratio, cladding costs constrain articulation, and overcladding creates bleak and flat facades, color offers an opportunity for expression and articulation of program. At 10 Montieth Street in Brooklyn, designed by ODA, powder-coating aluminum window frames in red, orange, and yellow creates a distinctive ombré facade. At The Aya, by Studio Twenty Seven Architecture in Washington, DC, color wraps rooms, demarcates community space, and organizes the navigation logic of the floors. New investment in color is coupled with a rise in formal articulation and part-to-whole relationships in large multifamily projects, as at Independence Library and Apartments, designed by John Ronan Architects. There, distinctly colored balconies celebrate the individuality of the different families housed within, intentionally rejecting Chicago's history of bleakly homogenized public housing. Amid the abundance of neutral palettes that have flooded housing design, these projects signal a shift: expression is on the rise, with color as its mascot.

Partial Isometric Elevations

a   Independence Library and Apartments, John Ronan Architects, Chicago, IL
b   The Aya, Studio Twenty Seven Architecture, Washington, DC
c   10 Montieth St., ODA, Brooklyn, NY
d   Edwin M. Lee Apartments, Leddy Maytum Stacy Architects, San Francisco, CA

Adaptive Renovations

There is a new urgency for the rehabilitation of older housing structures driven by diverse needs, including climate adaptation and mitigation, preservation of modest and affordable homes in the face of limited new supply, and changing demand for both residential and commercial spaces. Notable projects surveyed have transformed former schools, motels, office high-rises, and retail strip malls. These projects exemplify trends in both urban densification and building envelope sealing and insulating. Also notable is designers' engagement with residents, many of whom are empowered to contribute sweat equity and/or are able to stay in place during repairs— a crucial metric for social success in these projects. An increase in federal, state, and local funding programs has spurred much of this innovation.[i] Similarly, states are increasingly using carrot-and-stick policies to push their existing stock of buildings ever closer to net-zero (see the New York Local Law 97[ii] and the Massachusetts Clean Energy Center[iii]).

Although building reuse can be more costly than ground-up construction, designers are seeking to change that developmental calculation in favor of saving the embodied carbon in existing structures and unlocking more interesting spatial possibilities that come with found conditions. Several projects showcase how designing a building to stay put—when under threat of gentrification or climate change—can promote efficiency, equity, and justice. Mainstream design efforts, such as the American Institute of Architects (AIA)'s statement on the Green New Deal,[iv] have also shifted the field's attitude toward renovation as a primary practice model. Retrofitting may finally be "cool" again—thanks, in part, to celebrated work like that of recent Pritzker Prize laureates Anne Lacaton and Jean-Philippe Vassal of Lacaton & Vassal, who are known for renovating public housing in France. In an era where cost and culture severely limit the production of new housing structures, projects in densification, carbon sequestration, and domestic transformations are critical for the viability of the cities and neighborhoods in which we live. In her essay, Adele Peters uncovers the pressures and possibilities within existing buildings, outlining retrofitted housing in New York; Portland, Oregon; Moorhead, Mississippi; Santa Ana; Los Angeles; Chicago; Philadelphia; and Somerville, Massachusetts.

---

i   HUD's HOME Investment Partnerships Program; Environmental, social, and corporate governance (ESG) funds; RetrofitNY; HUD SNAPS funds, etc.
ii "Compliance," "Violations for Non-Compliance," "Violations for Non-Reporting," https://www.nyc.gov/site/sustainablebuildings/requirements/compliance.page.
iii "The Challenge: Rapidly Scale All-Electric Retrofits of Small, Multifamily Buildings," https://www.masscec.com/program/triple-decker-retrofit-pilot.
iv "AIA Supports Green New Deal Framework," https://www.aia.org/press-releases/6105450-aia-supports-green-new-deal-framework-.

by Adele Peters

Until last summer, an affordable apartment building in Brooklyn's Bushwick neighborhood looked like any of the other 1990s-era developments that pepper the area. But within a few months, it was transformed. A sculptural white facade, made of eight-inch-thick insulation, now covers the exterior, with a new heating and cooling system incorporated onto the walls. The building now meets Passive House standards and is expected to cut energy bills by 80 percent.

The building, part of a series of retrofits by the nonprofit owner RiseBoro Community Partnership and architect Chris Benedict, is one example of the type of work that will have to happen at a massive scale to meet climate goals. Buildings are responsible for 27 percent of global emissions during operation; more than 70 percent of the current housing stock in the US will likely still exist in the middle of the century, when the world aims to hit net-zero emissions. At the same time, as housing demand continues to grow, renovating existing buildings—and adapting offices and other commercial space into apartments—can help avoid some new construction and the additional "embodied" carbon in new materials. And as American housing stock ages, repairs are also needed for livability. RiseBoro's work, like the eight other projects profiled in this essay, illustrates how this type of design continues to evolve.

Benedict's angular, raised facades draw attention to the insulation, something that she says is often overlooked, compared with "green" features (like solar panels or green roofs) that have less benefit. "Part of my work is to create an iconic look for buildings that have gone through this type of transformation," she says.

RiseBoro has now completed similar retrofits on eight other buildings, including five that were a century old and used inefficient oil-fired steam heat. "Energy drove our decision-making process," says Ryan Cassidy, the nonprofit's director of sustainability and construction. As heating and cooling bills shrink, the tighter walls also reduce mold and pests and improve air quality. A state program, RetrofitNY, helped fund the work as a pilot project. Cassidy, who wants to replicate the process at other properties, says that one challenge now is to convince future lenders that the work makes financial sense, despite a higher upfront cost. But as long-term owners and managers, the company sees the work as essential both for its mission of keeping housing affordable and meeting climate goals.

Although renovation and adaptive reuse are common in market-rate housing, other affordable housing owners are also finding ways to finance the work. Nearby, in the Bronx, a public housing project built in the 1960s called Baychester Houses used funding unlocked by the federal government's Rental Assistance Demonstration (RAD) program for an extensive renovation in partnership with private developers. Having never been properly waterproofed, the group of 11 buildings was deteriorating and infested with mold; the grounds were unsafe and filled with garbage. Developers spent two years reworking the property to save energy and improve living conditions, with new cladding, repairs to roofs and HVAC systems, new lobbies and other common spaces, security cameras, and apartment renovations that were carefully managed so that tenants didn't have to move out as the work happened.

> The residents, accustomed to broken promises, were skeptical about the process. The team prioritized work inside apartments so that residents could see changes happen quickly. They also met with tenants to understand their biggest concerns, including security. "They listened to us," says Sandra Gross, resident association president at Baychester Houses, who has lived in the complex for 28 years. Tenants also questioned whether they'd be evicted so that rents could be raised after the repairs, but that hasn't happened; the units have a requirement to remain affordable, with residents paying no more than 30 percent of their income. L+M Development Partners, one of the firms that led the project and manages the property, now brings residents from other public housing developments for tours to make the case for similar conversions.

In Portland, Oregon, the city's housing authority, Home Forward, also worked with the federal RAD program to renovate several properties to improve energy efficiency, quality of life, and operational costs. Most of the buildings, built between the mid-1960s and early 1980s, had deteriorating exteriors and issues with mold. Five have now been transformed by the architecture firm Holst. One of the buildings, for example, now has a new building envelope and an HVAC system, insulation, heat recovery ventilation, LED lights, a solar hot water system, and a green roof and bioswales to manage stormwater. It's expected to last another 50 years. Another building has multiple new terraces and a revamped community space.

> Like the RiseBoro buildings and Baychester Houses, the Home Forward retrofits also include new cladding to make the buildings airtight and improve energy performance. In each case, the changes seem like an unambiguous improvement; the original architect for one of the complexes, Gallagher Plaza, called the Holst team to thank it for completing work

that the initial team couldn't afford. But as retrofits of older buildings become more common, they also raise questions about aesthetics. When does it make sense to cover a historic brick facade, for example, and how much should new designs reference the original building? Other approaches may emerge. In France, the architects Lacaton & Vassal retrofitted social housing with enclosed balconies that give tenants new outdoor space and more light, while also adding insulation without new cladding.

Some other renovations are tackling groups of single-family homes. In Mississippi, a development of dozens of affordable homes called Eastmoor Estates was built in 1969 outside the town of Moorhead—a location chosen because it meant that Black residents would not be able to vote in town elections—and it quickly deteriorated. The county and city shared responsibility for infrastructure, but both neglected the area, as did the developer who rented out the homes. The street frequently flooded, and when it rained, raw sewage seeped into some yards and bathtubs. After a few decades, foundations were failing and roofs rotting. Electrical issues caused fires. A congressman eventually intervened, and the owner lost tax credits and Section 8 subsidies. The residents, all people of color, also later sued and forced the local government to repair the road and sewer system. In certain cases, because some tenants had entered into unfair lease-purchase agreements with the developer, the developer was forced to deed over the homes to those residents.

Delta Design Build Workshop, a local social impact firm, partnered with Hope Credit Union, a local bank that secured a grant from Goldman Sachs to rehabilitate 44 homes for owner-occupants. Delta did major repairs where needed and fully replaced 14 of the homes. For others, the team painted and made smaller upgrades, such as adding new cabinets. It also audited the homes' energy use and closed air gaps and added insulation, helping households save an average of $170 a month on energy bills. The changes have also impacted the health of residents, including a young baby who had been repeatedly hospitalized because of mold in one of the homes. "The baby didn't have lung issues or chronic asthma—it was fully an environment issue," says architect Emily Roush-Elliott. "I think architects, as a profession, identify with aesthetics, but we actually have so much power to impact people through the environments we're creating."

As the housing shortage continues, and renovation alone can't meet demand, a rising number of nonresidential buildings are being repurposed as housing. Although the trend has accelerated since the pandemic emptied out offices, it was already growing. In Santa Ana, California, an underused five-story office building built in the 1960s was recently

Adele Peters

Home Forward's renovated Sellwood Center is now home to occupiable roofs with planter beds and gathering space.

New townhomes at the Santa Ana Arts Collective fill the corner of the existing mid-century office building site.

Delta Design Build mainly works in and hires from the Mississippi Delta, where it claims that the problem is not a lack of housing stock, but rather deteriorating stock and appraisal gaps that make investing unfeasible.

A courtyard at La Placita Cinco opens up and steps down to the adjacent neighborhood.

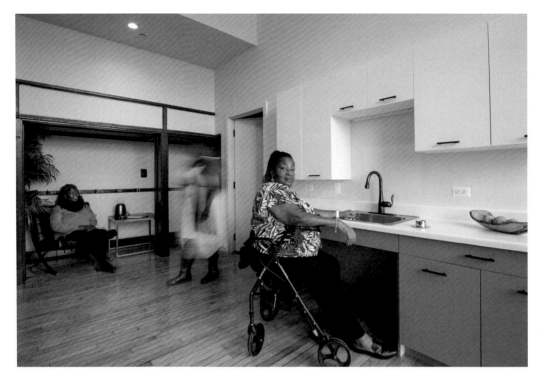

The West Pullman School Senior Housing complex combines modern interior finishes with the restoration of unique trim and built-ins.

The courtyard at Huntingdon Mills both engages the street and creates a new space for gathering.

Adele Peters

converted into affordable live-work lofts for artists, who began moving into the space in 2020. The project, called the Santa Ana Arts Collective, made seismic improvements and added new insulation, cladding, and glazing as offices were converted into townhouses of various sizes, with gallery space and a shared makerspace on the ground floor.

The architects calculated that reusing the building avoided more than 2,000 tons of CO_2 emissions and diverted 25 million pounds of waste from landfill. Because the apartments require fewer parking spaces than offices, the developers were also able to use part of the surface parking lot to build additional townhouses. The location is within walking distance of a museum and other cultural spaces in the city's downtown; part of the funding came from a state climate program in support of affordable housing that makes it possible for residents to drive less.

The project was the first built under an adaptive reuse ordinance that the city passed in 2014, modeled on a similar ordinance that Los Angeles used to repurpose old buildings. Other conversions are underway, and more are likely to follow as remote work continues and more companies choose not to re-sign commercial leases. Nationally, the number of office-to-housing conversions jumped 43 percent between 2018–2019 and 2020–2021.[1] In California, the state government recently set aside $400 million in grants for office conversions.

[1] "New Data Reveals the Growing State of Adaptive Reuse Residential Conversions Nationwide," https://archinect.com /news/article/150329918 /new-data-reveals-the -growing-state-of-adaptive -reuse-residential -conversions-nationwide.

The projects are typically faster than building from scratch and can be less expensive. They also tend to face less comunity opposition, says Michael Bohn, senior principal for Studio One Eleven, which designed the new space. Although neighbors might fight a new five- or six-story apartment building, adapting a building that's already standing faces much less risk of the "not in my backyard" objections that have helped slow the growth of new housing in the state.

In some cases, developers leave some retail stores in place while adding housing. In another part of Santa Ana, an aging strip mall built in the 1970s—with a laundromat, grocery, locksmith, and other small businesses, along with a sprawling parking lot and a former gas station on the corner—was slated for demolition. A developer planned to tear down the stores and rebuild. But when a tenant with a long-term lease resisted, the plans changed, and the nonprofit Community Development Partners bought the developer's share to build affordable housing for artists instead.

The new design, called La Placita Cinco, added new facades, signage, and larger overhangs to the stores; it also upgraded the mechanical systems and added cool roofs to the buildings. A new mixed-use building with 50 affordable apartments and community space on the ground level replaced the gas station. Murals painted by local artists help

The units at Huntingdon Mills include lofted and nested elements that read as insertions into the existing structure.

point to the history of the community. After a negotiation with the city to reduce parking requirements, a small park was added between the buildings, along with wide sidewalks and space for a farmers' market. The mid-century layout, designed for driving, was rethought for a time when more people want to be able to walk or ride the nearby light rail.

"We basically took that auto-centric circulation that was once required for the car and gave it back to the pedestrian," says Tim Mustard of TCA Architects, which worked on the space with design studio City Fabrick.

Other renovations creatively reuse historic buildings. In Chicago, the West Pullman Elementary School closed in 2013 as the number of students in the area fell. Built in three phases, between 1894 and 1923, the school was designated as a historic landmark and couldn't be demolished. Scott Henry, a local developer whose mother and grandmother had attended the school, decided to convert the space to senior housing after the firm's market analysis revealed a need for affordable housing for older residents, particularly veterans. UrbanWorks converted former classrooms into spacious apartments with chalkboards and coat hooks intact, along with student cubbies repurposed as personal storage.

The school's original large windows fill the rooms with light, although as in other adaptive reuse projects, the architects had to find ways to work with spaces that couldn't easily be translated to housing. A former school restroom that the architects converted into a community space, for example, had high windows with no view outside. But the window placement "brings daylight deep into the space, creating an intimate place for neighbors to connect with one another," says architect Maria Pellot.

In Philadelphia, a former textile and yarn mill that spans two buildings was recently adapted by Interface Studio Architects into offices, a daycare, and loft-like affordable apartments that offer discounts for healthcare workers and make use of the original structure's high ceilings and large windows. A new addition links the two buildings with a staircase, an elevator, and three additional units and creates a third wall for an inner courtyard. The city originally developed with factory buildings interspersed with housing; as factories later closed and sat vacant, neighborhoods declined. Repurposing the buildings as housing can help strengthen the community while also giving new residents access to walkable neighborhoods near transit.

In Somerville, Massachusetts, another former elementary school, built in the 1960s with a bunker-like concrete design, was closed in 2004 because it was underused and expensive to maintain. When the city called for proposals to redevelop it in 2015, most plans suggested tearing it down. The winning architects, from Sebastian Mariscal Studio, met with community members who wanted to preserve the

Terraces, circulation, and courtyards overlap at CALA, peppered with landscaping and murals.

collective memory of the school while adding green space to the neighborhood. The final mixed-use project, called CALA (Community-Architecture-Landscape-Art), opened in 2020. It reuses most of the building's original structure, exposing concrete beams, while peeling away outer walls to let light into apartments and offices. Murals fill some of the original buildings' windowless walls. The former paved playground is now a public park that leads into a courtyard and roof garden. "The idea really was to try to break that boundary between private and public," says studio head Nina Gonzalez.

2   "Renovation Claims 50% Share of Firm Billings for First Time," https://www .aia.org/articles/6502007 -renovation-claims-50-share -of-firm-billing.

The majority of architecture firm billings now come from renovation rather than new construction, according to an AIA survey in 2022.[2] Still, fewer than 4 percent focus on improving energy performance. Policy changes can help begin to shift that. In New York City, for example, most large buildings will have to meet new energy efficiency standards by 2024,[3] with a goal to cut emissions from those buildings by 40 percent by the end of the decade. (Buildings covered by the law will need to file certified reports about their performance.) Boston and Washington, DC, have similar building performance standards. That's forcing improvements and pushing contractors to quickly learn new skills. New York City also recently formed an adaptive reuse task force to explore the potential for housing in old office buildings.

3   "Local Law 97," https://www.nyc.gov/site /sustainablebuildings /ll97 /local-law-97.page.

The developers and architects who are doing this work want to do more and say that more funding is necessary. The new Inflation Reduction Act can help, with up to $8,000 per unit available in energy retrofit rebates for multifamily building owners and additional funding available for affordable apartment buildings. The infrastructure law passed in 2021 also has expanded funding for weatherization. "As an owner and manager, we're in these communities helping them thrive for the long term," says RiseBoro's Cassidy. "And so we see these types of renovations as critical to that mission. It's critical to making affordable housing stay affordable—and also for climate goals."

Adaptive Renovations Projects

Typical Floor Plans

■ Dwelling Unit

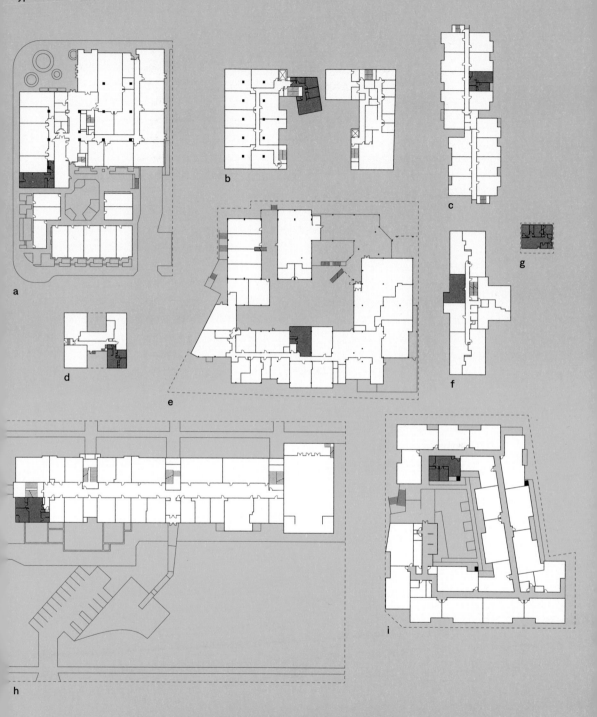

a   Santa Ana Arts Collective, Studio One Eleven, Santa Ana, CA
b   Huntingdon Mills, ISA, Philadelphia, PA
c   Gallagher Plaza, Holst Architecture, Portland, OR
d   RiseBoro Community Partnership retrofits, RiseBoro, Brooklyn, NY
e   CALA, Sebastian Mariscal Studio, Somerville, MA
f   Baychester Houses, Curtis + Ginsberg Architects, Bronx, NY
g   Eastmoor Estates, Delta Design Build Workshop, Moorhead, MS
h   West Pullman School Senior Housing, UrbanWorks, Chicago, IL
i   La Placita Cinco, TCA Architects, Santa Ana, CA

Farmhouses and Spaceships

Corrugated metal cladding and fiber cement panels have become popular contemporary cladding choices, valued for their low cost, lightness, ease of installation, durability, and ascetic aesthetics. Cold-rolling and bending metal sheets adds rigidity to an inherently thin material. On the exterior, the effect adds a deeper texture than could be achieved at the same price from thicker materials. Facade motifs range from the much-desired "farmhouse" aesthetic (Myers' Home) to the chic warehouse (C-Channel Lofts) and the faceted and fractured (Orange Crush, Dillon617). Fiber cement, by contrast, is an inherently formless composite that offers a more resilient and maintenance-free alternative to typical wood siding. Panels range from those mimicking lap siding to custom shapes and profiles, with a limited range of greiges and blacks or painted in color-blocking primaries. Some projects resist the Hardie-metal dichotomy, such as Scott's Grove (by LDa) or Cable Mills (by Merge Architects), who embrace cedar wood siding for its natural resistance to wear and the gray-tone patina it develops over time. Others, such as Rig-A-Hut and the Rose Mixed-Use Apartments (by Brett Schulz and Brooks+Scarpa, respectively) employ fileted and fluted coverings, playing with light and shadow through subtle surface texture. Ultimately, metal and fiber cement panels offer uncompromising low cost and depth. And, when coupled with larger building footprints—as cities trade setbacks for density and developers look to maximize their lots—buildings that use these panels have been hailed as spaceships touching down in the neighborhood. Although other materials may front the primary facade, building entrance, or ground floor, metal and fiber cement can fill in the gaps elsewhere—providing scaleless coverage in any shape, size, orientation, or pattern.

Materials Legend

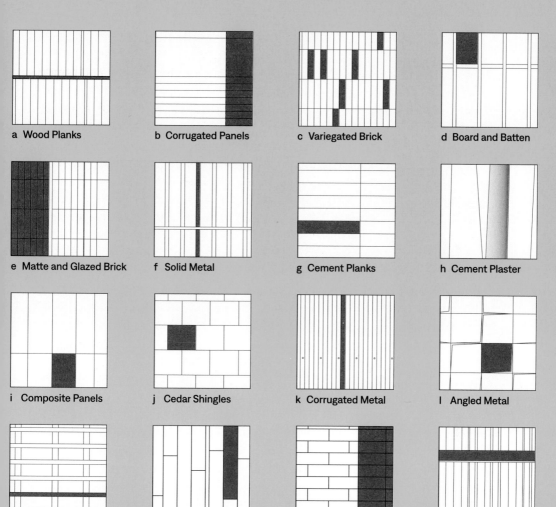

a Wood Planks

b Corrugated Panels

c Variegated Brick

d Board and Batten

e Matte and Glazed Brick

f Solid Metal

g Cement Planks

h Cement Plaster

i Composite Panels

j Cedar Shingles

k Corrugated Metal

l Angled Metal

m Wood Lattice

n Cedar and Fiber
   Cement

o Enameled Brick

p Corrugated Metal

a	C-Channel Lofts, Michael Etzel, Portland, OR
b	Orange Crush, ISA, Philadelphia, PA
c	222 Taylor Street, David Baker Architects, San Francisco, CA
d	Finley Street Cottages, Kronberg U+A, Atlanta, GA
e	The Louisa Flowers Apartments, Lever Architecture, Portland, OR
f	Dillon617, LOHA, Los Angeles, CA
g	Willowbrook, Lehrer Architects, Los Angeles, CA
h	Rose Mixed-Use Apartments, Brooks+Scarpa, Venice, CA
i	ReCenter, BRAVE Architecture, Houston, TX
j	Scott's Grove, LDa, Martha's Vineyard, MA
k	Myers' Home, Rural Studio, Newbern, AL
l	Rig-A-Hut, Brett Schulz, Washougal, WA
m	Fir Street Flats, Westerbeck Architecture, Bothell, WA
n	Cable Mills, Merge Architects, Williamstown, MA
o	1490 Southern Boulevard, Bernheimer Architecture, Bronx, NY
p	Taylor Street Apartments, SOM, Chicago, IL

Collective Capital Stack

Creativity in finance can sometimes generate more innovative housing models. For example, in many projects we surveyed, small-scale housing developers have turned to crowdsourcing to build their capital stack.[i] (The 2012 JOBS Act, which made advertising crowdfunded investments legal, and Securities and Exchange Commission [SEC] amendments in November 2020, which increased the maximum offerings that can be exempt from SEC registration, have prompted an increase in crowdfunded real estate.) Low-entry, low-risk shares allow individuals to invest as little as a few dollars into a project,[ii] promoting broader funding sources and enabling residents to pitch in to (and benefit from) local development. Jolene's First Cousin, a retail and residential building by Brett Schulz Architect, was designed for mixed use, including subsidized housing and retail spaces, with help from individual investors who accepted a lower return on investment than typical financing. Similarly, at Bungalow Gardens, by Restore Neighborhoods LA, whose goal was to provide transitional housing for people experiencing homelessness, a portion of the equity was crowdsourced and delivered by 57 individuals. Finally, the Travelers Hotel in New Orleans, designed by OJT, incorporates the sweat equity of resident artists who deliver hospitality services in exchange for reduced housing and studio space fees. The project was initially funded through crowdsourcing and today is managed by a collective, which furnishes and oversees the spaces communally, lending their personal and artistic touches to what is often a cold and anonymous typology. Although crowdsourcing mostly remains only a portion of a project's total funding, participatory investment can help drive a project's stated social mission, especially when said mission is eschewed by typical lenders looking for the lowest-common-denominator product.

---

i   Housing projects are financed by what is referred to as a "capital stack," some combination of financing sources that include traditional construction loans, mortgages, private equity, federal and state tax credits, specific grants, etc.

ii   Although similar to real estate investment trusts (REITs), which have been one way for retail investors to get involved in development, crowdsourcing operates through platforms such as SmallChange, a web-based service that allows potential investors to browse for projects based on categories (e.g., women- or minority-led developments, affordable housing) and provides easy-to-read metrics (e.g., a project's mission, location, and return-on-investment rates). REITs, however, tend to operate at a distance and usually through many opaque layers that disconnect the investment from place and purpose in favor of distributed risk.

■ Percent of Funding
Crowdsourced

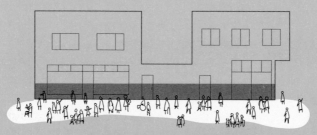

a　14% crowdsourced from +/- 43 investors

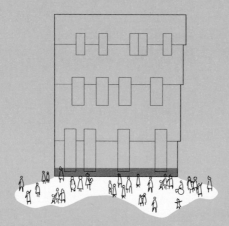

b　5% initially crowdsourced from +/-31 investors

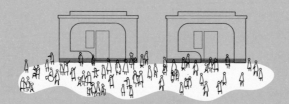

c　7% crowdsourced from +/- 57 investors

a　Jolene's First Cousin, Brett Schulz Architect, Portland, OR
　　$300,000 Crowdsourced
b　Travelers Hotel New Orleans, OJT, New Orleans, LA
　　+/- $111,000 Initially Crowdsourced
c　Bungalow Gardens, Restore Neighborhoods LA, Los Angeles, CA
　　$100,000 Crowdsourced

Creating Context

At the largest scale of housing development, projects are designed from the beginning to create their own context. The value-driven potential of these developments often relies upon using undervalued or transitioning urban land (rail yards, industrial zones, waterfronts, brownfields). However, these areas tend to be disconnected from the surrounding community fabric, and thus their designs often look inward for identity, connections, and character. At their best, these developments provide abundant new housing and resident resources, regenerating what are often ecologically damaged sites. With very long implementation timelines, any analysis of these developments must take into account the shifting political, climatological, and market spheres in which they take shape. At scales ranging from 7 to 700 acres, the best developments modulate scale through typological aggregation. Others fail to create a character that integrates into the existing city or community and, at worst, contribute to displacement and profiteering. Still, in using housing as a tool to generate a new sense of context, developments—benefiting from expanded community feedback processes—are becoming better able to contribute to repairing the urban fabric.

Emphasizing distinct identity, whether real or imagined, can also complement developers' branding efforts. Programmed landscapes and careful circulation accentuate design attention toward unique open spaces, neighboring-unit relationships, and phased implementation. "Verde" and "Village" are monikers of a marketing strategy to convey how homey and green new developments are meant to be. Exacerbated by work-from-home trends following the COVID-19 pandemic, developments with on-site amenities are also marketed with the ubiquitous "live, work, play" mantra meant to invent the idea of a mixed-use city feel, without necessarily the corresponding density. Projects that create their own context—played out in detached developments and super-blocks—do not fight the friction of a torn urban fabric but reorient communities inward, with hopefully adequate resources to match. In her essay, Marianela D'Aprile explores the scale and situation of urban housing developments in Austin, Detroit, the Bay Area, and New York.

by Marianela D'Aprile

American cities, even the densest of them, have a tendency toward large-scale blankness. With most development in this country driven by for-profit enterprises, cities, or at least parts of them, are prone to falling into disrepair, or laying idle despite the need for housing and common spaces, if fixing or developing them won't prove economically profitable. This blank-slate quality of much American urban and suburban development generates the need for large-scale building that forges an identity all its own. In many of these cases, developers are left to make their own rules. By creating context in this way, they are also able to attempt to solve multiple problems—not just that of blankness—at once. The projects discussed in this piece have this in common: they attempt to fill multiple programmatic needs, as well as fill out large swaths of space, even as they primarily provide housing. They do so via similar means, but because they each address specific, unique problems, those means are almost always deployed to different ends. Rather than inquire about the degrees of success of each intervention, it's more interesting to identify the conditions to which each of them responds and the effects produced by each of their self-created contexts.

In New York City, two projects use large-scale development interventions to attempt to create a sense of place for communities at risk of displacement. "Place-making, what makes a place, is important to us," Christian Bailey, principal at ODA, told me. ODA designed the 500-unit building 10 Montieth in the Brooklyn neighborhood of Bushwick. The development, which occupies a full city block, combines 300 market-rate and 100 affordable units into a single building designed in a figure-eight shape, with two internal courtyards that are visible from the street level and a roof level that is accessible from every residential floor. "The activation of the roof is a theme throughout all of our work," Bailey told me. "It has only gotten more important since COVID. We've been doing it for years and it has been recognized as successful, and now we are seeing more and more demand." More than simply providing an amenity, the accessible, programmed roof of 10 Montieth serves to reinforce the connection between the building and its surroundings, allowing people to travel from it to the street and to look out onto wide views of the neighborhood. Inside, affordable and market-rate units are interspersed throughout, the building's finishes working to create a single aesthetic identity for all of the units, no matter their target

The activated roof on ODA's 10 Montieth is accessible from every residential floor and provides views over the neighborhood.

Given 10 Montieth's full-block dimensions, ODA was able to incorporate an ample community courtyard in the center of the building

resident. "We wanted to avoid having a separate wing or a separate space for affordable units," says Bailey. "Only some finishes might be different; they really look and feel similar to the rest."

The building's full-block footprint and its material palette (metal panels, some in bright sunset colors) help to set it apart from the neighborhood, bolstering a sense of self-contained community, while its outdoor spaces create a connection to the neighborhood—all strategies used by another New York City project, Sendero Verde in East Harlem. The 100 percent affordable, 709-unit development also occupies a full city block, breaking up its mass into three buildings that react to the different conditions at each edge of the site: a 35-story tower on the northwest side of the block, away from the train tracks that abut its eastern side; a 15-story building on the north side of the block; and a 10-story building on the south side that avoids casting additional shadows onto the street. The material finish on the outside, familiar brick masonry, helps to link the building materially to others around it, while its unique, vertical configuration helps to set the development apart from an older New York City Housing Authority (NYCHA) development to the north. Louis Koehl, senior associate and director of sustainability at Handel Architects, told me that "there was a big concern about the NYCHA buildings to the north," referring to a seven-block, towers-in-the-park-style development whose outdoor spaces are not well integrated and whose brick exteriors with small, square windows seem impenetrable from the street. Koehl told me Handle wanted to "make sure that what we were putting in the community was not a repeat of that." Outdoor spaces between the three buildings and on the corners of the site help to create connections between the building and passersby and make up for a lack of outdoor space in the immediate area. "Central Park is close, a few blocks away, but in terms of a more six- or eight-block neighborhood kind of park, there is not anything in the area." Similarly, 10 Montieth provides a grocery store in an area that was once a food desert.

Although filling in gaps in amenities seems a priority for these urban developments—whose users are less likely to use a car and therefore need services that are accessible by foot or via public transportation—similarly scaled developments in less dense contexts take on different goals. In Detroit, a car city par excellence, a development named City Modern attempts to provide housing while rehabilitating old, abandoned sites. With much of Detroit's housing stock in disrepair and new residents lured downtown by low real estate prices, there was a need for a development that would put forward a template for interacting with the existing architectural context. City Modern does not intervene on the scale of the master plan at all, instead building within Detroit's existing fabric. The project introduces twenty new buildings and renovates four existing houses within three blocks of Detroit's Brush Park neighborhood. Some of the buildings look like the large-scale, mixed-use, five-over-one developments you might find in any other growing city, while others innovate with form by reinterpreting such typical Detroit typologies as the carriage house. Going by its overall form, City Modern's primary concern seems to be figuring out how to introduce new buildings into a complicated, if neglected, urban fabric. The development's varied texture is mediated by its public-facing presence; a website and other marketing materials boast amenities and lifestyle under a single brand.

Branding is a crucial aspect of context-creating via architectural and urban means. Creating a new context ensures that a development will have a cohesive identity. Underscoring this cohesion via branding helps to reinforce an identity that can then be used to attract new residents and investors. "A groundbreaking development made up of residences that soon will include restaurants and retailers," says City Modern's website. In Austin, Texas, a development called Mueller promotes itself as "transit-oriented" and "pedestrian-friendly."

This new development promises a place to live and plenty of space for those who want to stay in the city but have been priced out of developments closer to downtown. It takes its name from the Robert Mueller Municipal Airport that once occupied its site and recalls earlier New Urbanist developments, like Seaside, Florida, and Disney's Celebration. There are single-family homes for sale; there are apartments for rent. There is a man-made lake, a museum, a grocery store, a pool, a farmers market, and restaurants and stores along Aldrich, the street that delineates Mueller's residential area to the Northwest. There is a hospital, a greenway, a wine shop, and even a hotel for people visiting from out of town. It's a small town in a big city, with many amenities available if not within walking distance—sidewalks, where they exist, appear mostly unshaded, a dangerous quality in a city where the 2022 high was 110 degrees Fahrenheit—then within its borders.

There's something strangely homogeneous, almost Stepford-esque, about Mueller and top-down developments like it. With a single developer whose eyes are on the bottom line, setting the standards for what gets built and what doesn't and what things look like, it's easy for such places to replicate the sterile quality of many American tract suburbs, with only a veneer of "place" provided mostly by stores in which to spend money. The near-simultaneous nature of the development—everything completed within the span of a few years—also adds to the development's uncanny quality, its shiny-new houses and parks and streets evoking a movie set or Disneyland's Main Street. Still, the development takes previously unused land and uses it to

Handel Architects split their 760-unit Sendero Verde project into three buildings of different heights, differentiating the massing from a nearby NYCHA complex and allowing for communal open spaces throughout the development.

provide housing to a city that has received an influx of new residents over the past ten years—33 percent population growth between 2010 and 2020, according to its chamber of commerce. Rents in Austin have gone up significantly in the same time frame; a study by Zillow shows that the total amount of rent paid by Austin tenants increased 92.6 percent between 2010 and 2019.[1]

[1] "U.S. Renters Paid $4.5 Trillion in Rent in the 2010s," https://www.zillow.com /research/total-rent-paid -2010-2019-26112/.

Spearheaded by for-profit developer Catellus, Mueller promises that 25 percent of both its for-sale and for-rent homes will be affordable, reserved for people making 60 percent of the area median income. And although there is an overall sense of sameness, the development retains some variety, as the parcels have been filled in by different developers and architects—including one stretch of 11 row houses developed by Habitat for Humanity and designed by Michael Hsu Office of Architecture.

Across the country, in California, a development in the town of Patterson sets up a similar sense of community, but for an entirely different set of residents. Patterson is a predominantly suburban town, populated in large part by agricultural workers. Stonegate Village, a development led by Self-Held Enterprises (SHE), provides a mix of housing types for a variety of target residents. Among the development's 260 units, there are single-family homes, apartments for sale and for rent, and shared community amenities. SHE, which developed Stonegate as part of Villages of Patterson, was at least partially spurred by the desire to provide housing for local residents to prevent Patterson from becoming a bedroom community for Bay Area residents who were being priced out of San Francisco, Oakland, and Berkeley. "The sense we got from the community in Patterson," project manager Miguel Arambula tells me, "is that they wanted units so that their own residents wouldn't be priced out of the community. They didn't want to see the affordable, available homes going to people from outside, so that people who lived there for generations couldn't find a place for themselves. A lot of it was making sure that people who had lived in the community for a long time had a place to stay." Developing a cohesive identity, both via design decisions and through a program in which future residents participate in building their own homes, was a way to achieve the goal of creating a self-contained community that would reinforce a sense of place for Patterson locals—and no doubt a reaction to the aggressive real estate development that threatened that sense of place to begin with.

For each of these projects, the creation of context serves a distinct purpose. For 10 Montieth and Sendero Verde, it helps to provide a sense of identity for their resident communities, but it's also born of necessity, of making up for existing deficiencies in their respective surroundings. For Mueller and City Modern, it helps to establish a new formal language in places where old forms no longer serve a

City Modern includes both new construction and renovated historic buildings, integrating housing into Detroit's existing urban fabric.

Located on the site of a defunct municipal airport, Mueller incorporates both housing and a number of amenities, including restaurants, grocery stores, and a museum.

Marianela D'Aprile

The Stonegate Village development is designed to cultivate a sense of place among residents while preventing the town of Patterson from becoming a high-cost bedroom community for the San Francisco Bay Area.

Stonegate Village comprises 260 housing units, including both apartments and single-family homes, as well as community amenities.

useful purpose. And, in Patterson, creating new context contributes to deepening a sense of community against real estate interests that might threaten existing residents. In most of these cases, context-creating is virtually a necessity, not a totally free design choice but rather a reaction to conditions that cannot be changed. And, as in the case of Mueller, City Modern, and even Stonegate Village, a cohesive, easily explainable identity created by a strong, self-defined context is also good marketing. "Your urban oasis, your city sanctuary," 10 Montieth's website boasts. Many of the decisions that forge these developments' unique identities—from the provision of affordable housing at Patterson and the rehabilitation of the Mueller airport site to 10 Montieth's grocery store and Sendero Verde's outdoor spaces—are often correctives for the effects of abandonment and disinvestment—making up for neglect and for a lack of architectural cohesion, public amenities, and affordable housing. They're perfectly fine reactions to existing limitations, and most of these developments are even successful at filling in the gaps. This is valuable for residents, and maybe even for neighboring inhabitants, who might benefit from additional services and amenities. At the same time, these projects' self-created context also risks isolating them from their surroundings. It's a danger that architects seem aware of— but it might not be able to be fully mitigated through design.

■ Urban Anchoring Element

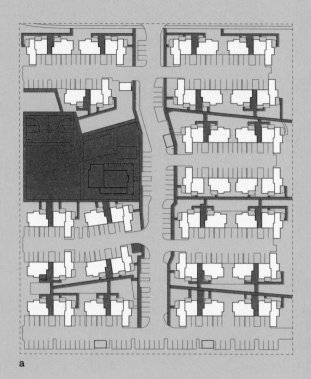

a

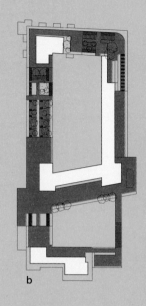

b

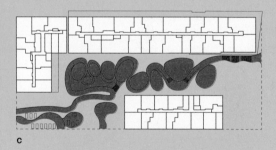

c

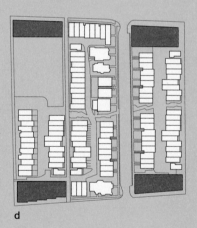

d

a Stonegate Village, Mogavero Architects, Patterson, CA
b 10 Montieth (The Rheingold), ODA, Brooklyn, NY
c Sendero Verde, Handel Architects, New York, NY
d City Modern, LOHA, Detroit, MI

Emergency Villages

Tiny homes and micro-villages have emerged as a short-term response to people facing unsheltered homelessness in urban areas. Often sited on leftover, oddly shaped, non-strategically-located parcels (often publicly owned) that developers have overlooked, tiny home villages nonetheless require the same range of infrastructure, zoning, engineering, and certifications that a midrise, multifamily building might. Sometimes constructed onsite and sometimes prefabricated and shipped, the small structures that make up these villages combine the intimacy of a campground with the intensity of an urban context. The tenure of these developments is unclear: often sold to the public as temporary, most have no expiration date or permanent alternative in progress. At Lehrer Architects' Chandler Boulevard Bridge Home Village in Los Angeles, supergraphics in the form of colorful pavement, facades, and fences bring local artists into conversation with trucked-in PVC and light-gauge sleeping units. The fully electrified, conditioned, ready-for-use projects are intended mostly just for sleep—living and community amenities exist elsewhere onsite. At Tiny House Empowerment Village in Oakland, by Youth Spirit Artworks, youth-designed tiny houses frame miniature mews, providing homes, job training, and mentorship for homeless youth. At the Cottages at Shattuck, by ICON Architecture, 20 units were constructed in just 100 days, providing much-needed relief for individuals who previously lived at an informal street encampment. The white-gabled huts cluster in a high-fenced enclosure at the periphery of a state-owned medical complex, adorned with polygonal graphics, wooden furniture, and planter boxes. At a tiny house village in Seattle, homes are partially designed and built by the Environmental Works Community Design Center, local vocational and training programs, and private architecture firms. The clusters operate as a self-managed community, embedding cooperation into both the architecture and maintenance of these temporary places. Although philanthropy[i] or governmental decree[ii] enable the quick implementation of these projects, their ability to thrive will depend on whether the organizations and communities can work together to fight for a place in the city.

i   "Arnold Schwarzenegger Donates 25 Tiny Houses to Homeless Veterans," https://nypost.com/2021/12/30/arnold-schwarzenegger-donates-25-tiny-houses-to-homeless-vets/.
ii "A Look Inside the Shattuck Cottage Community," https://www.commonwealthcarealliance.org/about-us/newsroom-publications/a-look-inside-the-shattuck-cottage-community/.

Site Plans

■ Housing
□ Communal Services

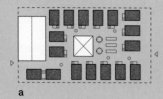

a

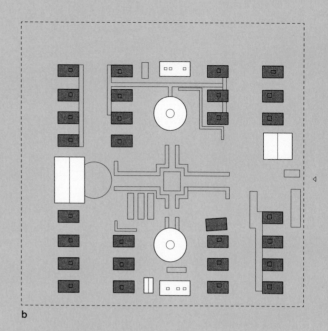

b

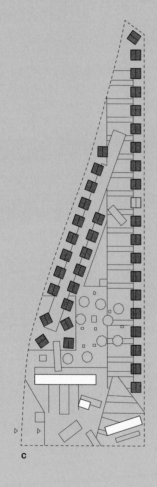

c

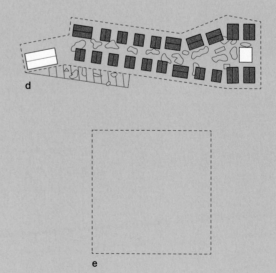

d

e

a   Tiny House Villages, EWCDC, Seattle, WA
     15 Units
b   Tiny House Empowerment Village, Youth Spirit Artworks, Oakland, CA
     26 Beds
c   Chandler Boulevard Bridge Home Village, Lehrer Architects, Los Angeles, CA
     39+ Units
d   Cottages at Shattuck, ICON Archtiecture, Boston, MA
     20 Units
e   Median Single Family Lot Size

Pre-Approved Plans

Many cities are looking for new ways to directly support small-scale neighborhood housing development. One trend has been the production of pre-approved designs, typically provided for free by the city or directly through local architects for a small fee. Although the plans recall the Sears and Roebucks kit homes that could be purchased from a catalog, what's new is the fact that cities themselves are now designing and publishing drawings, an approach that reflects municipalities' efforts to reduce the financial cost of approvals and the lengthy period they often take. For example, Eugene, Oregon, offers four ADU designs by local architects (for purchase at a flat rate) and one by its own planning office that can be modified with a shed or gable roof, and a large or small porch. The set is 14 drawings, complete with structural illustrations to facilitate construction (although each sheet has a disclaimer limiting the city's liability and implying a need to formally engage the requisite professionals before applying for a permit). Los Angeles commissioned 39 architecture firms to produce 72 pre-approved ADU designs, each ultimately owned by those firms. The city's own design, YOU-ADU, comprises 21 pages certified by the city engineering department and local consultants. Developers or homeowners are given a sheet with checkboxes for customization that range from sprinklers to cladding choices. (A disclaimer stipulates that the model may not work for every site and that additional review may be required to evaluate its context.) Finally, South Bend, Indiana, has produced a catalog of seven urban housing types rather than an exhaustive set of construction drawings. The types, each with sub-variations for different densities, illustrate for public and professional audiences the kind of missing middle housing the city is seeking to encourage.

Pre-Approved Plans Processes

Model
Options

Drawing
Set

Design
Choices

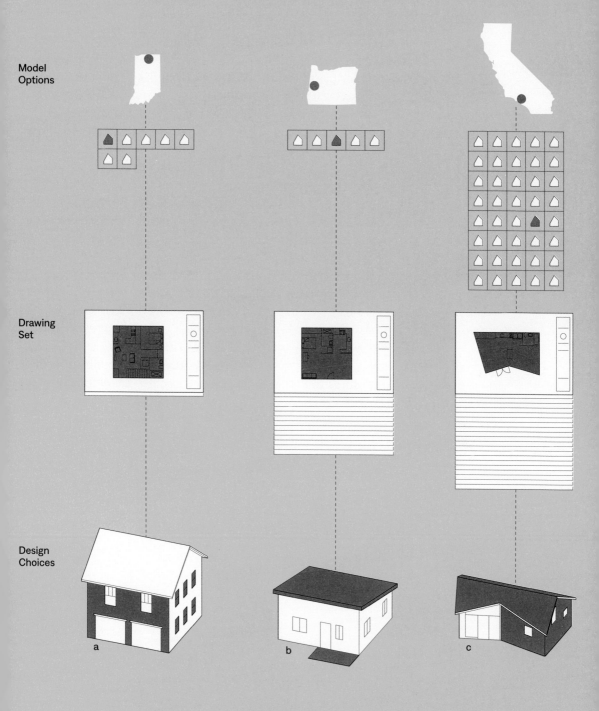

a   Carriage House, City of South Bend, South Bend, IN
b   EOR ADU, City of Eugene, Eugene, OR
c   YOU-ADU, City of Los Angeles, Los Angeles, CA

Creative Corridors

Housing design operates under some of the stiffest development constraints in the building industry, usually with a high efficiency standard[i] and strict control of exterior envelope exposure.[ii] Hallways, stairs, and elevators are thus typically minimized as much as possible and tucked in the interior of the plan to save valuable exterior wall surface. Although a plethora of alternate arrangements exist for high-density circulation, none matches the ruthless efficiency of the double-loaded corridor: the ubiquitous housing layout of a hallway with units on both sides. As the floorplan game is played out by countless development and design firms nationwide, the result is often dim, repetitive, and unfriendly to the human character. Several notable projects from the past several years disregard this template and expand their circulation to perform as more than a connection between the building's front door and the individual unit's futon.

The architects of selected projects widen their central axis, kink passageways, bring halls outside, bank common programs along routes, and cover collective spaces with partial screening, all to bring more light, air, and life into the journey around one's greater home. These strategies appear in projects of low-rise, mid-rise, and high-rise densities. However, such innovation is inhibited in some geographies by stringent local codes and the constraints of fluctuating climates (keeping emergency access routes clear of clutter and safe from weather). In addition, the legacy of many mid-century social housing projects unfairly demonizes the exterior walkway. Double-loaded corridors are the result of fire safety codes mandating two stairs—particularly American phenomena—and while American architects lead public dialogue questioning the necessity of these codes,[iii] other countries may be moving to add a stair for fire safety.[iv] In his essay, Charles Shafaieh walks the halls of projects in Los Angeles, New York, and Senatobia, MS, challenging the path of least resistance.

i   This standard typically aims to achieve 75–85 percent efficiency, which measures leasable or livable space versus space for common infrastructure, such as equipment rooms, stairs, corridors, mechanical chases, and walls.

ii   In multifamily buildings, in particular, where minimum living room widths, bedroom window exposures, emergency egress codes, and accessibility standards come into play, each room competes for maximum exterior envelope. At the same time, this envelope is one of the costlier elements of construction, making the ratio of exterior surface to floor area another dialectic metric that illustrates housing's architectural and developmental conundrum.

iii "June 23, 7pm: Cancel the Corridor," New York Review of Architecture, https://newyork.substack.com/p/june-23-7pm-cancel-the-corridor.

iv "Sprinklers in care homes, removal of national classes, and staircases in residential buildings," Department for Levelling Up, Housing & Communities, https://www.gov.uk/government/consultations/sprinklers-in-care-homes-removal-of-national-classes-and-staircases-in-residential-buildings/sprinklers-in-care-homes-removal-of-national-classes-and-staircases-in-residential-buildings#paragraph-106-and-107--call-for-evidence.

by Charles Shafaieh

The double-loaded corridor, a ubiquitous feature in American multifamily homes, is miserable. Dimly lit and claustrophobic, these passageways, in which apartments flank both sides, cannot be traversed quickly enough by residents. This dismissive attitude is not their fault, though; these spaces are cast aside before design begins. Incentivized by profit, developers typically seek a 75–80 percent efficiency rate for housing projects, meaning at least three-quarters of any building is delegated to the units themselves. The units' square footage can be marketed and sold, unlike lobbies, stairwells, gardens, or open rooftops, which must be maintained at a financial loss or billed as common charges. Among the predictable cost-saving results are corridors that feel more like concealed pipes which funnel contents from Point A to Point B as quickly and discreetly as possible.

Humans are not water or waste, however. And although designing for speed epitomizes the etymology of "corridor" (*currere,* Latin for "to run"), it ignores the holistic experience of living wall-to-wall with sometimes hundreds of other people.

"I believe human beings are inherently social. I tend to think that's what makes life worthwhile, and architecture plays a significant role in facilitating interaction," says Lorcan O'Herlihy, whose firm has offices in Los Angeles and Detroit. A native of Dublin, Ireland, O'Herlihy cherishes the dynamism of the European piazza, replete with people-watching and chance encounters between diverse populations. Counterintuitive though it may seem, he advocates recreating this energy in housing: common spaces become simulacra or extensions of city streets, dissolving the notion of the apartment as a solely private sanctuary.

At two of his Los Angeles projects—MLK 1101 and Granville 1500—the demarcation between private and public space blurs from the first engagement with the sites. For both, O'Herlihy used dramatic triangular folds at the property edge that pull pedestrians into adjacent cuts, where the entrances are located. At MLK 1101, a 26-unit supportive-housing site, the cut takes the form of an exterior staircase that climbs to a fenced entrance, which leads to a stoop. "The goal was to pull back the security element from the street and open up the building, to let everyone know they have a right to be on this development," he says. Especially important for a formerly unhoused population, who are often treated as invisible or explicitly ostracized, this injunction to see and be seen serves as a form of social equity and justice. Additional visibility is created

LOHA's emphasis on the single-loaded corridor opens the courtyard to residents for visual and physical interaction.

throughout the property by single-loaded corridors bound by units on one side and, on the other, porous fences that look onto an interior courtyard. There, a large residents' garden and social area adjacent to a community room encourage gathering.

At Granville 1500, the triangular folds also lighten the impression of a potentially imposing facade. Grandiosity is further avoided by a design featuring three volumes rather than one. The cuts here lead to vast public courtyards, surrounded by unit windows and balconies as well as open-air bridges between buildings. "The question was: How do you design an urban village? How do you design a parti where the strategic cuts provide outdoor spaces that combine circulation with opportunities to gather?" says O'Herlihy. "The sidewalk becomes a space to hang out, as opposed to a conventional walkway."

Similarly, at Kevin Daly Architects' Gramercy Senior Housing, the linear interior spine that connects all six pieces of the site functions as a space for stasis rather than only movement. Each of the 64 units in the Los Angeles project has a private terrace that flares into this extended corridor, which also features larger shared meeting spaces. These inverted balconies (as they are positioned inward rather than toward the street) originated, in part, as a solution to the apartments' compactness. "Because these are intimate spaces—one-bedroom units with a living-dining-kitchen space—the level of privacy that people want to maintain isn't going to allow others to be invited in at any time, as you're cooking and living in one place," explains Daly, who has offices in Los Angeles, New York, and Miami. "Those circumstances generated these outdoor living rooms where you can visit your relatives, be outside, and build a social space that would make a more thriving community. It's the elderly, affordable version of the dorm, where you can leave your door open."

The apartment blocks do not align along the corridor, to prevent windows from directly facing each other. This affords the terraces a degree of privacy. Simultaneously, sight lines are multiplied due to the lack of symmetry, in addition to the partly transparent facade and the latticed balustrades that trace through the site. "That was intentional, to make sure people feel they can see activity, such as when your neighbor comes home," says Daly. SO – IL takes porousness and visibility further at 450 Warren, an 18-unit site in Brooklyn that, like Granville 1500, comprises three volumes. Although an elevator exists in a small glass enclosure at the building entrance, the staircase in the large interior courtyard provides a more inviting journey. "Normally, egress stairs are hidden, but we wanted to make something that would stimulate people to walk actively into the building," says Florian Idenburg, cofounder of the Brooklyn based firm. Within this space, residents are greeted by a contrapuntal series of rectilinear and curved walkways

MLK 1101's staircase stoop exemplifies the residents' reciprocal relation to the street.

Granville 1500's curved and corrugated panels frame the buildings' courtyard.

which allow natural light to interact with the space in unpredictable ways. Furthermore, the light is reflected by a transparent mesh net that encloses these walkways and replaces both walls and handrails, allowing greater visibility and encouraging interaction. "We've always been interested in this mesh and in playing with the straight versus the curvilinear. Here it creates a dramatic effect and less regular experience, so it becomes more adventurous to move up through the building."

Another type of circulation is a constant concern for Idenburg. Cross-ventilation is enabled by coupling the courtyard and the units' windows that look into it with each apartment's multiple balconies. Despite the challenges of implementing this passive design strategy in New York City, Idenburg considers it essential. "The New York City energy code doesn't allow for passive cooling, and the renewed regulation is pushing more and more for hermetically sealed buildings rather than those that breathe," he says. In other words, it favors buildings that include double-loaded corridors. The COVID-19 pandemic made air circulation a more pressing issue, however, which is why firms like O'Herlihy, Daly, and Idenburg's—all of which already advocated cross-ventilation—have not needed to change tactics since 2020. "People were very comfortable in the streets and in their homes but were uncomfortable in the in-between spaces," says Idenburg. "This project tries to do that differently." As if this health incentive were not enough, cross-ventilation drastically reduces energy consumption and provides a haptic connection with the outdoors, as birdsong and street chatter travel through the apartment along with the air.

Like Daly and O'Herlihy, Idenburg designs for stasis as much as for circulation. At 450 Warren, each unit has a variation on the front porch, with a bench, where residents have ended up putting strollers, umbrellas, or shoes. "Although it's a common space, everybody feels it's theirs," he says. These spaces help make more gradual the move from home to street, from private to semi-private to public spaces. Akin to the interventions of the aforementioned projects, they change one's rhythm, compelling people to slow down and linger, whether they are conversing with someone else or not.

Roy Decker employs this strategy, which he calls "pause and move," throughout his residential and institutional projects alike. In doing so, the cofounder of Duvall Decker, based in Jackson, Mississippi, seeks to redefine the corridor— its purpose and the experience of it. "In a pause-and-move plan, every pause has an inner horizon of multiple choices. You enter a space, and there are, say, two or three different directions, maybe some views, and then you go further into the depth of the building, where you have three more views. You can make a whole building with this plan,

Layered with vegetation, Gramercy's central spine opens in certain areas to exposed courtyards.

Kevin Daly Architects designed interior living spaces that merge with inverted balconies and larger shared meeting spaces beyond.

The open-air corridors of SO-IL's 450 Warren provide semi-private spaces that help slow the transition from street to interior.

The three volumes of 450 Warren huddle around the interior courtyard, which hosts the curvy building circulation.

Charles Shafaieh

and you won't ever realize you've been in a corridor, which is simply a moment of delaying or expanding choices," he says.

This agency is particularly critical at the Baddour Center, a residential facility for people with intellectual disabilities in Senatobia, Mississippi. While researching this population, Decker learned that some residents could be very affected by loud noise, like air conditioners, or surprises, such as somebody coming around a corner unexpectedly; they also might disturb a conversation by simply walking directly into a room, potentially causing an altercation. Sensitivity to these conditions produced numerous design decisions which reinforce how passageways can act as a means to preview spaces that someone may not want to enter. For example, Decker designed a pathway from the residents' bedrooms to the outside that is adjacent to the kitchen-dining-living area without pushing its occupants into the space itself. After previewing this common space, a person can choose to move in a straight line outside the building and not engage anyone else. At the same time, he or she is visible to anyone inside that room. Other subtle features that emphasize the pause-and-move rhythm include material, color, and elevation changes at thresholds.

Whereas corridors have historically been a tool of surveillance, whether the boulevards of Haussmann's Paris or those in schools and hospitals, at the Baddour Center authority is dismantled as power is given to the residents. The design lets them determine whether they want to cross thresholds and creates a choice of having chance encounters. Caregivers do not have offices, which eliminates their panoptic presence. "Most architects reapply the structures of authority without thinking about them," says Decker. "The corridor plays a secondary role and is very maze-like. You are in-between—but not in a celebrated in-between, not in a place where you have choice. For twenty years, we have been working on understanding how we fall prey to a control society. Here, the authority figure is dismantled out of the architecture so that they are just a visitor in the house."

By creating "a celebrated in-between," each of these architects seeks to bring together members of a divided and individualistic society. As inspiration, Decker cites Richard Sennett, who criticizes the siloing of our communities and the decreased role colleges and other institutions play in challenging our identities and value systems, and in introducing us to a wide array of people. "To an extent, that's an architectural problem," Decker argues. "How do we intentionally create opportunities for conversation?" Daly explicitly employs the college-dorm ideal at Gramercy Senior Housing, whereas Idenburg and O'Herlihy create nooks, crannies, and larger courtyards that make connecting with neighbors not only a possible choice but an appealing one. In each instance, the implicit injunction is the pause that Decker advocates.

Creative Corridors

The elbow of the Baddour Center floorplan provides crucial sightlines for residents.

Duvall Decker designed pathways that continue to the outside, some of which terminate at a covered porch.

Charles Shafaieh

Despite 450 Warren having about a 55 percent efficiency rate, the developers took a risk and financed it. They discovered that people were willing to pay more for the square-foot price of their units because they understood and appreciated the generosity of the surrounding design. Even the client calls it home now. "This has to do with the way we value things," says Idenburg. "We often tend to talk about how big an apartment is and the cost per square foot—things we can quantify. It's very hard to talk about the unquantifiable. But the units sold before the building was finished. People understood there was value in shared open walkways that enhance connectivity with your neighbors and in generous windows that create a strong relationship to the environment."

About 40 percent of O'Herlihy's clients negatively highlight the need for more exterior-access walkways to service units in single-loaded buildings, yet he is convinced that the lighting, insulation, and HVAC requirements of a double-loaded design will be equal in cost to, or more expensive than, this alternative. He believes that he has been more successful than many of his peers in getting developers to change their priorities, but it remains a struggle. Perhaps more than the disincentivization of profit among developers, the move to single-loaded corridors requires a larger cultural shift. Americans may have become too accustomed to seeing the home as what Idenburg calls "a cocoon of amenities"—a view he thinks must be eradicated—and instead should be more connected to the environment, even in colder climates. O'Herlihy is convinced the transition away from the double-loaded corridor can be successful anywhere, based on the positive responses he has received for similar projects in Detroit. "The home needs to offer comfort," says Idenburg. "But it also connects us to others and the space we inhabit on this planet."

Creative Corridors Projects
Typical Floor Plans

■ Corridor

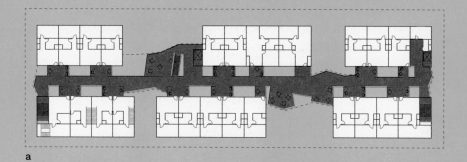

a

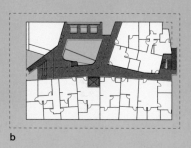

b

c

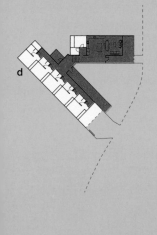

d

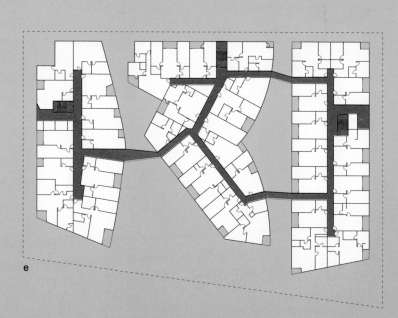

e

a   Gramercy Senior Housing, Kevin Daly Architects, Los Angeles, CA
b   MLK 1101 Supportive Housing, LOHA, Los Angeles, CA
c   450 Warren, SO-IL, Brooklyn, NY
d   Baddour Center Transitional Home, Duvall Decker, Senatobia, MS
e   Granville 1500, LOHA, Los Angeles, CA

Get to Zero

The most fundamental shift in environmental design over the past few decades has been in how we respond to climate change, with increased efforts to reduce the carbon footprint of buildings by improving the building envelope and reducing energy demand. When it comes to regulations, many certifications and standards have emerged that seek to streamline knowledge and compliance and incentivize architects and builders to adopt carbon-reduction technologies. These include LEED, PHIUS or PHI (Passive House), Green Globes Building Certification, Living Building Challenge, Zero Carbon Certification, Enterprise Green Communities, Fitwell, WELL, Green Communities Criteria, Energy Star Certified Building, the 2030 Challenge, and the NBI Multifamily Building Guide. Moreover, certain states and cities have developed aggressive regulations to track energy use, improve building performance, and subsidize new technologies. Architects have responded with tighter and thicker envelopes, more continuous insulation, and passive design features. At the Front Flats in Philadelphia, Onion Flats designed a multifamily structure fully clad in solar panels. The black volume pushes energy production beyond a fifth facade gesture or offsite compliance path into a brise soleil skin that provides shading and captures solar rays. Blokable at Phoenix Rising provides high-efficiency units constructed in modular fashion through a vertically integrated development, design, and build company. At St. Peter Residential, a multifamily project by Eskew Dumez Ripple in New Orleans, an articulated ground floor contrasts with an opaque primary facade of restrained apertures meant to lessen the solar heat gain of units; the solar array battery storage system is proudly displayed on the designer's website. Although zero-energy projects often embrace high-tech imagery of systems and surface articulation, embedded carbon in existing buildings is key. The Owe'neh Bupingeh Preservation Project, by AOS architects in Ohkay Owingeh, New Mexico, pays attention to that aspect, restoring part of a 600-year-old pueblo in consultation with Ohkay Owingeh elders and tribe members to generate new, efficient housing through mud plaster techniques.

■ Resilient Design Feature

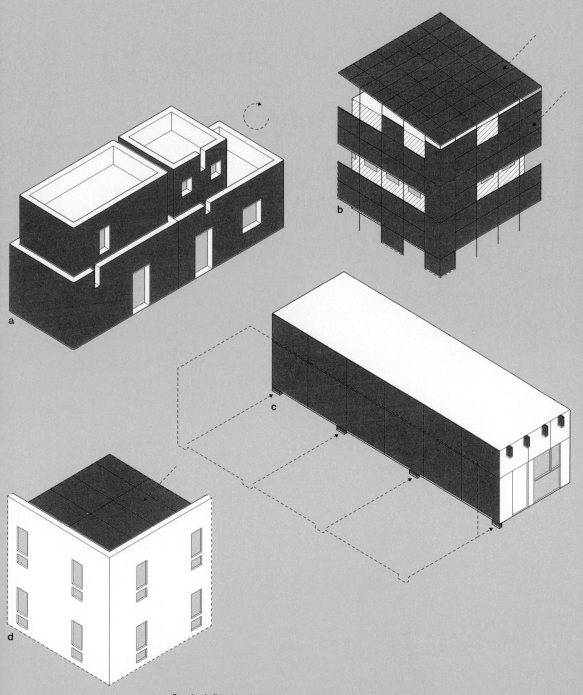

a   Owe'neh Bupingeh Preservation Project, AOS, Ohkay Owingeh, NM
        Adobe preservation and rehabilitation using local, indigenous
        materials and construction methods

b   Front Flats, Onion Flats, Philadelphia, PA
        Translucent solar panels as building skin that double as solar
        shading and offer visual privacy

c   Blokable at Phoenix Rising, Blokable, Seattle, WA
        Structural connectors for modular construction for multiunit
        attached infill project

d   St. Peter Residential, Eskew Dumez Ripple, New Orleans, LA

        450 solar panels

Housing Beyond the Home

Models following the theory of "housing first,"[i] "the first 72+,"[ii] or "rapid rehousing" seek to provide unconditional shelter for those who need it most, including unhoused people, former or currently substance-addicted people, elderly people, disabled people, and people reentering society after incarceration. Designing for these populations typically entails incorporating spaces for a variety of services, including addiction treatment, employment assistance, onsite nursing, and group therapy, not to mention study space, communal kitchens, and gardens. For example, the Ivy Senior Apartments in San Diego, by BNIM, houses seniors with chronic medical needs who have experienced homelessness and is influenced by trauma-informed tactics and the materiality of the local Southern California context, resulting in dual single-loaded rows of rooms, buttressed by open-air corridors that surround a central courtyard. Under similar programmatic constraints, the Tahanan Supportive Housing project, by David Baker Architects, used modular construction to achieve rapid assembly in an urban infill context. Inside, a double-loaded corridor is flanked by handrails for mobility support and recessed unit entries with pastel highlighting. The Meadowlark in Missoula, Montana, by MMW Architects, also embraces color through primary blocks of domestic motif volumes. A playground, communal kitchen and dining area, lounge, and youth area serve the needs of up to 44 families, many of whom are seeking refuge from domestic violence. Finally, One Flushing, by Bernheimer Architecture in Queens, New York, uses subtle gradations in brick color to subdivide a massive 400-foot-long facade enclosing 230 units of intergenerational housing. A vertical sawtooth motif breaks up long strings of tightly packed units, whose efficiency allows for more expansive communal spaces, an adult day care center, and outdoor gardens. Handrails, seating heights, and lighting levels exemplify interiors that aim to meet residents' needs and inspire delight at the same time.

i   "Housing First," https://endhomelessness.org/resource/housing-first/.
ii   "The First 72+," https://officejt.com/work/the-first-72-housing-for-the-formerly-incarcerated
     -new-orleans-louisiana-us/.

Programmatic Sections

+ Health and Wellness
🌿 Community Garden
🛋 Lounge and Community Space
🖌 Training and Education
♥ Supportive Services
▦ Employment Opportunities
🔒 Retail Units
✕ Communal Kitchen

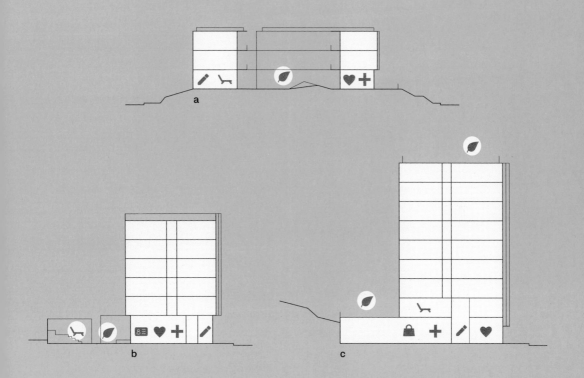

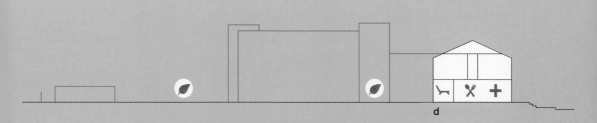

a   The Meadowlark, MMW, Missoula, MT
    31 Units
b   Tahanan Supportive Housing, David Baker Architects, San Francisco, CA
    145 Beds
c   One Flushing, Bernheimer Architecture, Queens, NY
    230 Units
d   The Ivy Senior Apartments, BNIM, San Diego, CA
    52 Beds

Modular, Panelized, and Pre-Made

Modular construction for multifamily and single-family dwellings has become increasingly diverse in recent years. Despite the continued predominance of standard on-site construction, off-site fabrications are ever present in our kitchen cabinets (IKEA), floor panels (cross-laminated timber), wall assemblies (shop-built and delivered), bathrooms (shower-tub units), and HVAC systems (heat pumps). Two-dimensional elements, such as floor and wall panels, promise decreased on-site construction costs as a result of more design coordination up front. Three-dimensional modules, such as kitchens, bathrooms, and entire dwelling units, further minimize site elements, with the caveat of much more up-front coordination, control, and decision-making than is typical in the design-bid-value engineer-build process. These modules and flat panels are designed to the logistical limits of a truck bed and benefit from the climate-controlled space in which they are fabricated. Although the speed of construction may not differ radically from site-built buildings, it is the pace of staging and assembly where these systems have proven to further reduce hard construction and soft land costs. The labor involved also shifts from the field to the factory, raising economic impact issues around local union involvement and job creation.

      The ability for design to unlock modular cost savings matters less for the individual project than for a series of projects. This has spawned a series of vertically integrated companies—developer/builder/architect/engineer—hoping to capitalize on a solution that is mass-produced. Prefabricated designs appear most in architectural typologies of either few or extreme site constraints. Since the most rational building volume misses some opportunities in the standard oddly shaped plot of land, the choice is whether to choose sites where the losses are negligible or where prefabrication can achieve extra value through density. Today's prefabricated housing looks less repetitive or boxy than one might imagine, with many projects using their internal rigor to liberate a more contextual exterior. In his essay, Patrick Sisson traces the fast-evolving off-site construction and design industry through projects in Pittsburgh; Los Angeles; Portland, Oregon; Seattle; and Norwood, Colorado.

by Patrick Sisson

From the proliferation of early twentieth-century Sears Modern Homes kits and architect Frank Lloyd Wright's experiments with standardized designs to today's high-tech homebuilding startups, the mainstreaming of mass-produced and factory-built housing has always been a dream of the US construction industry. The connection between construction methodology and cost control—exemplified by the often overlooked role manufactured homes play in the housing market—has always invited experimentation. From 1969 to 1976, a large-scale Housing and Urban Development experiment called Operation Breakthrough deployed tens of millions of dollars to popularize new industrial methods of housing production.

Intensified struggles with housing affordability, shrinking construction labor pools, and more drawn-out and costly development processes have led many developers to give modular construction more serious consideration to meet this moment.

1   "Multifamily Developers Embrace Modular Building," https://www.constructiondive.com/news/modular-contiues-growth-in-multifamily/635930/.

Modular construction—the use of factory-made and assembled panels, walls, and even entire housing units, which are then transported and assembled on site, typically on the bed of a semi-truck—represents only a small (albeit fast-growing) slice of the overall industry. Roughly 5.5 percent of buildings were constructed this way in 2021, according to the Modular Building Institute.[1]

2   "Off-Site Construction in Los Angeles County: Unlocking theBenefits of Innovative Approaches to Housing Production," https://ternercenter.berkeley.edu/wp-content/uploads/2021/07/Los-Angeles-County-Off-Site-2021.pdf.

3   "Reinventing Construction Through a Productivity Revolution," https://www.mckinsey.com/capabilities/operations/our-insights/reinventing-construction-through-a-productivity-revolution.

But its advantages have generated considerable excitement, especially within the affordable-housing world. Modular production can result in higher-quality units, and more new builders have eschewed single-family projects for multi-family, which make up roughly a quarter of current modular projects. It's a process that also seems tailor-made to support the boom in accessory dwelling units. Most important, it saves significant time, a serious penalty in constrained and cost-restrictive coastal markets. A recent Terner Center study found that modular building cuts project timelines between 10 and 30 percent.[2] This time savings, for an industry that hasn't seen productivity gains for the past 75 years,[3] could be a game changer for housing, especially once the total volume of modular residential projects achieves economies of scale, including more efficient factories, reduced material costs, and more developed and expedited supply chains.

Clear signs of wider adoption have spread beyond the work of progressive architecture firms and factory startups testing and refining multifamily

Holst Architecture designed bright studio and bedroom units with natural finishes, filled with light.

A portion of the 287 units of housing constructed in Macon, Georgia through Operation Breakthrough.

Modular construction was used to construct 295 units of housing in Indianapolis, Indiana.

modular in urban centers across the country. PulteGroup,[4] America's third-largest homebuilder, and Greystar, a leading multifamily developer, are both investing in off-site manufacturing to buttress their businesses by increasing speed-to-market and cutting construction waste. The Biden administration has made investment in modular technology—and a push to simplify and streamline inspections and regulatory requirements—a part of its broader housing affordability agenda and has provided a $41.4 million grant for a mass timber modular demonstration factory in Portland, Oregon.[5]

4   "Your Next House Could Be Made on an Assembly Line," https:// time.com/6237782/modular -homes-affordability/.

But even successful examples of modular housing underscore many of the significant challenges the industry faces, including stifling local regulations, challenging funding arrangements, and an overall lack of a critical mass of factories, skilled labor, and customers needed for the industry to truly achieve assembly-line pace and precision, and achieve a real cost benefit without using traditional methods.

By its nature, modular design requires a more systematized and more up-front approach to design. Architects, already facing budgetary burdens, need to accept new limitations, such as how a housing module will fit and travel to the site on a flatbed truck, and the necessity of making every major design decision in advance. Designers and projects that treat these constraints as advantages can find new ways to achieve replication and reliably cut costs.

5   "President Biden Announces New Actions to Ease the Burden of Housing Costs," https://www .whitehouse.gov/briefing -room/statements -releases/2022/05/16 /president-biden-announces -new-actions-to-ease-the -burden-of-housing-costs/.

Golaski Lab Flats (2021), a mixed-use site at a former medical supply factory in a revitalizing section of Germantown, Philadelphia, added 35 one- and two-bedroom units in five-story stacked modular blocks adjacent to concrete and timber structures renovated for commercial use. ALMA Architecture principal Mathew Huffman compared the process of laying out the modules—a box-like assembly of bedroom, living area, kitchen, and bathroom accented in distressed wood and blue-and-white checkered tiles— to "designing for a submarine." But the project's budget constraints, specifically needing to fit a certain number of narrow units per floor, led to more vertical design strategies and subtle additions and tweaks that added volume, such as the placement of windows, exterior walkways, and balconies. The format ended up allowing for generous aperture and more public space at the front of each unit. Completed using New Markets Tax Credits in a federal Opportunity Zone in conjunction with impact developer Mosaic Developer, which plans to use modular methods again, it offers a potential blueprint for systemization.

On the other side of the state, in Pittsburgh, the Black Street Development (2020) served as a proof-of-concept for the flexible design system of hometown modular manufacturer Module. Set on a challenging sloped vacant lot—with a modular foundation system—the trio of homes hit different price points, including a two-bedroom affordable model, a duplex, and a market-rate three-bedroom home. The project showcased the firm's box model, where interchangeable floors, long and narrow to better fit urban infill lots, can be combined in various configurations. Removable roof systems allow owners to add stories when and if they desire, and the all-electric homes result in a more sustainable and healthy home with cheaper utility bills. "It gives you a sandbox in which you can be creative," said Module CEO and cofounder Brian Gaudio. "We're pushing the envelope in terms of materials and methods. There are some idiosyncrasies to figure out. But once you figure them out, you have a suite of tools that you can be creative with." The process also means that final design decisions get made up front, avoiding changes and in-process alterations that often lead to value engineering. Functioning as the contractor and manufacturer, Module cut the number of subcontractors needed by 80 percent, and by finishing six months earlier, shaved $30,000 off each home's total cost (the affordable model sold for $183,794). The firm focuses on working with impact investors—in this case, the Urban Redevelopment Authority of Pittsburgh and Bloomfield-Garfield Corporation.

Much of the excitement and hype around modular housing is happening on the more cost-burdened West Coast. In Los Angeles, Hope on Alvarado (2021), an 84-unit affordable development in the Westlake neighborhood by local firm KTGY, used a drop-and-lock method common to commercial building, with steel modules craned into place and slotted into a site-built concrete podium. That isn't to say the site looks repetitive or bland; the studio and one-bedroom units, with texturized facades of corrugated steel and exposed welds meant to exude an unfinished look, encircle a central courtyard, and the entire development boasts a shaded and landscaped rooftop deck. It was a system designed for customization; different units boast varying combinations of metal facades, vertical shades,

All three of the Black Street Development homes—from left; the duplex, affordable, and single-family homes—vary in square footage and bedrooms but share a material palette and street approach.

Hope on Alvarado's large courtyard provides community social spaces for its residents.

and interior windows to respond to their elevation and position. That flexibility and repeatability has allowed the firm to use the same system on three other ongoing projects: Hope on Hyde Park, Hope on Broadway, and Hope on Avalon. KTGY says the Alvarado project reached cost parity with traditional affordable projects.

A "kit of parts" approach informed the Argyle Gardens (2020) affordable development for single adults transitioning out of homelessness, designed by Holst Architecture. The Portland, Oregon, project built upon a set module that could be configured for workforce or student housing. Consisting of four buildings set on angles across the site, with four modules on each side—residents share kitchens, bathrooms, and common space to cut costs—Argyle features exterior walls of semi-transparent polycarbonate panels inset with brightly colored, patterned walls. Stick-built, illuminated staircases set behind the polycarbonate glow at night, and pitched roofs give each structure some added personality. Partly funded by a state grant that provided a tax break to affordable housing, the entire project was built and snapped together in eight months, yet it offers a more durable product than if built using traditional methods. Operator Transition Projects, an established nonprofit, can offer monthly rents as low as $295.

In Seattle, Heartwood (early 2023), an eight-story mass timber modular tower designed by atelierjones, will provide 126 units of middle-income housing for the Capitol Hills neighborhood for local nonprofit Community Roots Housing. Financed with a combination of conventional loans and private Opportunity Zone equity funding, the project is meant to address the missing middle housing challenge and uses unique wood-to-wood bearings and a perpendicular Glulam post-and-beam frame. A predominantly wood design, drawing from regional sources of hardwood, meant faster time-to-site for materials and enough room in the budget for an extra floor.

Architect Susan Jones said the key was elaborate planning to coordinate when the oversized timber panels were being put into place, as well as "embracing the logic of construction" to achieve the biophilic beauty and aesthetics tenants want—all while controlling costs. Within the building, visitors can see the different strains of tree via exposed interior beams, from Douglas fir to pine and spruce, providing a beautiful palette of colors within the building walls (it was built with a new structural code Jones helped author).

And in more rural pockets of the West, there are examples of modular projects tackling these regions' unique affordability challenges. Pinion Park (2022), a neighborhood development by Rural Homes in Colorado and the work of Wolf Industries, which manufactures tiny homes and accessory dwelling units (ADUs), points to the potential for modular processes to accelerate the growth in these alternative housing options. The firm is currently working on building a tiny home village in Vancouver, Washington, what it's calling a "town in a box." Founder Derek Huegel says the key to expanding the industry is more standardization, and perhaps having architects strive for more repeatability.

"Henry Ford offered only one color for the Model T when he started," Huegel said. "Before we can offer more options, we need to drive that cost down through increased capacity and standardization."

The movement toward more modular construction can get dismissed as a Lego-ization of housing, suggesting a bland, factory-made commodity, akin to the worst examples of ticky-tacky suburban boxes. But as the above-mentioned projects show, within the constraints of affordable, factory-built homes—which require expansive focus on the arrangement of hidden structures and systemic elements—there's room for design expression. Design can be a tool to unlock the potential of this process.

But the Lego metaphor, suggesting ease of assembly, also obscures the significant financial and material barriers facing the nascent industry. Lenders still struggle to understand the modular model and have difficulty shifting traditional mortgages to cover a modular home or ADU, said Tyler Pullen, a Berkeley researcher who studies modular housing. This is particularly challenging because, due to the compressed time frame and pre-built nature of modular homes, these projects require more up-front investment and rely on single suppliers who can't be replaced, adding more risk.

Present reality finds the industry stymied by a lack of clear guidelines and informed regulators. Regulations, and regulators, also often don't know what to do when it comes to modular factories or splitting inspections between factories and building sites. Some municipalities and states, such as California, are pushing for reform, but it's often difficult to be the first manufacturer in a particular market.

All these issues can create backlogs for new manufacturers and modular builders, which means that nascent factories, which depend on a steady flow of projects, have trouble staying financially viable over the long term. It's one of the reasons Katerra, which tried to bring modular techniques into the mainstream, crashed and burned, ultimately going out of business after scaling too rapidly. The trick is making modular more widespread. However, creating the infrastructure to support such a shift toward mass-market adoption—at a pace that matches the market's appetite for new projects—faces an uphill climb.

One of the 35 modular units is craned in at Golaski Lab Flats in Germantown, Philadelphia.

The steel modules for Hope on Alvarado were trucked to the site before being craned into place over a site-built concrete podium—a process that took one month to complete.

Patrick Sisson

Pinion Park in Norwood, CO offers workforce housing in rural Colorado to residents earning between 60 and 120 percent of area median income.

Despite the replication and repetitious nature of modular, design only becomes more vital to its evolution and success. Beyond the challenges of practicing architecture within these constraints, the overall design of delivery mechanisms—and systems that can be built to fit different lots and scenarios—creates an even greater and more complex task. But these hurdles seem more surmountable when considering the systemic challenges facing housing affordability and the way rising costs are pushing more people toward a similar conclusion. Even pessimistic viewers of the industry see that in markets like Los Angeles and San Francisco, realizing the value and benefit of modular, and unlocking the power of these designs, is more a matter of when than if.[6]

6   "Off-Site Construction in Los Angeles County: Unlocking the Benefits of Innovative Approaches to Housing Production," https://ternercenter.berkeley.edu/wp-content/uploads/2021/07/Los-Angeles-County-Off-Site-2021.pdf.

■ Pre-Fabricated Module

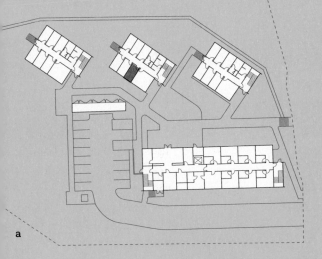

a

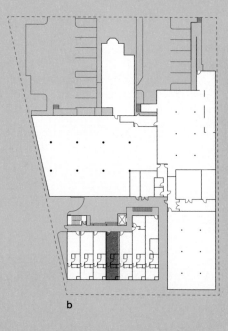

b

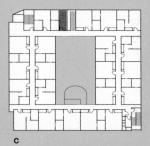

c

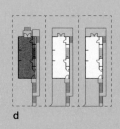

d

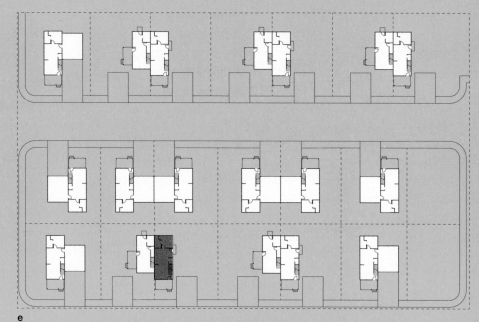

e

a   Argyle Gardens, Holst Architecture, Portland, OR
b   Golaski Flats, ALMA Architecture, Philadelphia, PA
c   Hope on Alvarado, KTGY, Los Angeles, CA
d   Black Street Development, Module, Pittsburgh, PA
e   Pinion Park, Rural Homes, Norwood, CO

Más Timber!

As of September 2022, 1,571 mass timber projects were completed, under construction, or in design in the US.[i] Mass timber, a category of engineered wood products made of compressed, laminated, or fastened layers of wood—typically produced in solid wall or floor panels, columns, or beams—can carry loads equivalent to those of steel and concrete, launching wood construction into a capacity beyond what light-frame and heavy timber construction has allowed in the past. The material is known to expedite onsite structural assembly, which balances its cost premium relative to steel or concrete. It also reduces carbon emitted during construction and sequesters carbon in the building itself (through the CO_2 the trees absorb in their lifetimes). Ascent in Milwaukee, Wisconsin, by Korb+Associates Architects, exemplifies the potential of wood, rising to 25 stories and over 280 feet. Like many forms of wood construction, this project hybridizes multiple systems to overcome the structural, height, or area limitations that a 100 percent wood structure would face, with the mix of cross-laminated-timber panels and glue-laminated-timber (Glulam) beams and columns sitting upon a six-story concrete and steel base. Other projects, like the Frame 283 in Brooklyn, New York, by Frame Home, surround twin concrete cores in wood to overcome regulations about shear strength and fireproofing. Pipes and conduits are exposed, since the solidity of mass timber leaves few cavities for critical systems, resulting in an industrial interior that this project embraces. Architectural coordination can often make or break construction of these units. In Timber House, by Mesh Architectures in Brooklyn, New York, the demarcation and coordination of where wood starts and ends, and where it is internally exposed, becomes a puzzle for designers to solve. Typically, we see living spaces and bedrooms with more exposed wood in their ceilings, walls, and structural members—a palette dictated by marketability but also building codes that strictly dictate the proportion of what is covered. The forests that supply the wood for these projects are being reshaped, stoking conversations between rural communities, timber companies, and conservation groups, who see many benefits to the rise of mass timber but also the need to track the carbon life cycle throughout the production chain and continuously improve the sustainability of forest management practices.[ii] In a country already making heavy use of light-wood framing, mass timber brings these supply chains into a high-tech construction process, with new intensity and implications for design processes.

i   This includes active projects in all 50 states of the US. "Designing and Building with Mass Timber: Design, Planning and Performance," Woodworks Wood Products Council, 2022.

ii   In January 2022, The Nature Conservancy released a new project, the global mass timber impact assessment (GMTIA), to assess the benefits and risks of mass timber's popularity. The GMTIA is a five-part research program that looks beyond building life-cycle assessments and includes global trade modeling to understand how timber supply and demand will affect forestry as an industry and ecosystem. "What Is the Impact of Mass Timber Utilization on Climate and Forests?" US Forest Service. See also "Do High-Rises Built From Wood Guarantee Climate Benefits?" https://www.invw .org/2020/05/04/scrutinizing-claims-that-high-rises-built-from-wood-fight-climate-change/.

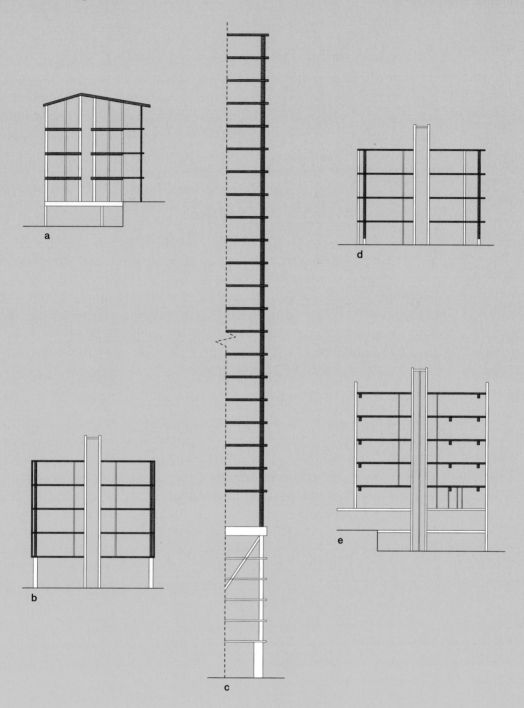

a   Chiles House, All Hands Architecture, Portland, OR
b   Juno East Austin, Ennead Architects, Austin, TX
c   Ascent, Korb+Associates Architects, Milwaukee, WI
d   Frame 283, Frame Home, Brooklyn, NY
e   Timber House, Mesh Architectures, Brooklyn, NY

Do-It-Yourself (DIY)

Construction is getting more complex every year. But because building things yourself can be cheaper and more flexible, many still choose the DIY route. For Rev. Walker's Home in Newbern, Alabama, Rural Studio drew from the tradition of expanding the home as wealth or family grows to develop a design that allows for long-term flexibility without compromising the initial structure and enclosure. Two metal-clad volumes are staggered on an expansive concrete pad, providing a platform for future projects on the currently oversized porch. The arrangement, resembling the Southern dogtrot home typology, is covered with a second gabled roof, open on all sides, with room for future additions. In the separate rural context of the Rio Grande Valley in Texas, MiCASiTA is a program to empower and assist families seeking more flexible financial tools to live securely in the present, while having room to grow in the future. Initial small loans for 600-square-foot starter homes are supplemented with education, financial counseling, and pathways for future loans—all for folks who do not qualify for traditional affordable-housing delivery models. Here, DIY means intimate resident involvement in selecting and modifying the home design—deciding which parts of the house should be built first and which parts should be saved for later. In Gustine, California, residents have been completing their own homes through the support of Self-Help Enterprises. The program, which pairs together 8 to 12 families, provides professional onsite supervision and jobsite training. Families work together to build each other's foundation, framing, wiring, enclosure, and finishes. Labor devoted is counted as part of the down payment, affording the opportunity for homeownership at a lower cash cost and with long-term benefits to homeownership maintenance and community. The DIY market share has shrunk over the past two decades, due partly to an aging and less able-bodied homeowner population. But metrics also point to the younger generation's zeal for DIY, along with the novel approaches to form, funding, and family housing it can provide. [i]

i   Harvard Joint Center for Housing Studies, *Improving America's Housing 2023*, https://www.jchs.harvard.edu/sites/default/files/reports/files/JCHS-Improving-Americas-Housing-2023-Report.pdf.

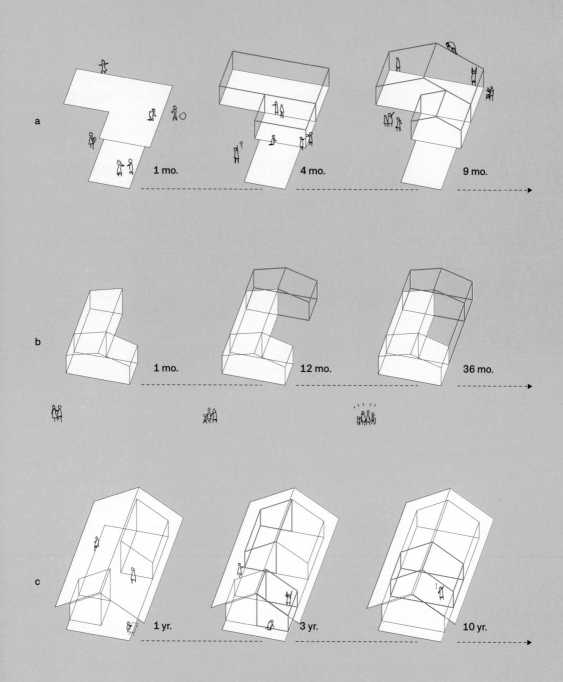

a — 1 mo.   4 mo.   9 mo.

b — 1 mo.   12 mo.   36 mo.

c — 1 yr.   3 yr.   10 yr.

a   Borelli Ranch, Self-Help Enterprise, Gustine, CA
        Communally built by families ten homes at a time.

b   MiCASiTA, BCWorkshop & CDCB, Brownsville, TX
        Built by module as family size and finance grows.

c   Rev. Walker's Home, Rural Studio, Newbern, AL
        Shell completed, with outdoor living and build-out potential.

Community-Led Development

In the current economic and political culture of US housing production, mostly a monotonous stock of single-family subdivisions or upper-end multifamily housing is being built. At all scales, these speculative developments are designed to be the least offending product, a criterion that results in less than stellar architectural outcomes. In contrast, some communities have turned to unconventional and more autonomous development approaches to design highly unique housing projects that address their specific needs.

These projects often start when resident groups partner with a developer or a housing authority—or, in some cases, self-organize—to design and build housing that is tailored to their ways of living. This process often drives a distinctive architectural outcome. Ownership and cost-sharing models for such developments range from cooperatives to co-housing arrangements. Architectural details are often subtle but rigorously planned to accommodate the accessibility and functional and programmatic desires of the residents, such as aging in place or general flexibility over time. Amenities are expanded to more supportive services and culturally aligned uses, such as collective kitchens, sewing workshops, or community health care.

From artists to people experiencing homelessness to Native American and displaced communities, residents across the US are using design to craft more personal expressions of home. These projects demonstrate the liberatory potential of community-led efforts to provide child care, spiritual connection to the Earth, and a heightened sense of security and independence through housing. In his essay, Stephen Zacks untangles the development pipeline for projects on sovereign Oglala Land in South Dakota; across Santa Fe, New Mexico; and in Southern California.

by Stephen Zacks

The design of homes and apartments well tailored to the specific needs of diverse community types and user groups has the potential to transform the policy debate surrounding public financing and subsidizing of affordable housing, creating the possibility of a crucial expansion of affordable housing in the US. With its sensitivity to the habits, belief systems, lifeways, needs, and desires of constituencies throughout the country, along with its efficient construction and effective maintenance, community-led housing should rebut arguments that have long precluded an adequate supply of homes to a substantial portion of the population ill served by the market.

Twentieth-century supply-side economists traditionally saw the role of government in offering housing in the narrowest of terms, arguing that rather than directly fund supportive, affordable, social, or public housing, the government should simply lower taxes, decrease regulation, and spur the private market to produce housing based on consumer demand. By 1999, the Faircloth Amendment fully adopted this principle into national policy by making it illegal for the federal government to increase the US public housing supply. Real estate developers argued that public housing would "crowd out" the private marketplace, suppressing demand for their output. The opposite happened: a private market serving less than half the population crowded out access to capital for projects serving the rest of the public.[1]

1   The average price of an existing home fell slightly in 2022 from $308,000 to $298,990, but prices remained high enough to require an annual household income of nearly $80,000 to purchase roughly half of the housing stock available in the country ("S&P CoreLogic Case-Shiller US National Home Price NSA Index," https://www.spglobal.com/spdji/en/indices/indicators/sp-corelogic-case-shiller-us-national-home-price-nsa-index/#overview). With median individual and household incomes in the US at $70,784 and $91,162, respectively, more than half of all households would not qualify for a home mortgage at those prices ("Income in the United States: 2021," https://www.census.gov/library/publications/2022/demo/p60-276.html; "Figure 1. Median Household Income and Percent Change by Selected Characteristics," https://www.census.gov/content/dam/Census/library/visualizations/2022/demo/p60-276/figure1.pdf; "Historical Households Visualizations," https://www.census.gov/library/visualizations/time-series/demo/households-historical-time-series.html). Meanwhile, national median rental prices rose above $2,000, putting the cost of attaining any kind of market-rate shelter beyond the reach of more than half of individual wage earners and nearly half of all households (Chris Arnold, "Rents Across US Rise Above $2,000 a Month for the First Time Ever," NPR, June 9, 2022. [This is based on the traditional calculation of annual income needing to be 40 times the monthly rent to qualify for a lease.]) In 2020, 46 percent of US renters were categorized as cost-burdened, spending more than 30 percent of their income on housing, including more than 23 percent spending more than 50 percent, according to the US Census Bureau ("Key Facts About Housing Affordability in the U.S.," https://www.pewresearch.org/fact-tank/2022/03/23/key-facts-about-housing-affordability-in-the-u-s/).

A variety of non-market-based alternatives attempt to fill the gap for millions of families, led by nonprofit community-led developers and supported by an uneven pastiche of government funding sources. Many of the programs originate at a hyper-local level, sustained by laws passed by state legislatures, city councils, and referenda of voters that aid in the development and provision of supportive services to homes and apartments at below-market rates. Nonprofit community-led developers typically finance projects by combining city, state, and federal grants, low-interest loans, and low-income housing tax credits with local, state, and federal rental vouchers, along with individual and corporate donations. Revenues from special funding programs for alternative energy and supportive services round out budgets for construction, maintenance, and operations.

> In affordable housing development, we should take "community" to mean not only the local citizens of an area and potential users of a building being served by the housing development, but all of the professional nonprofit developers and architects, elected officials and policymakers, public agencies, bankers, interest groups, and voters who facilitate or limit what a development in a community can constitute through their respective roles in design, production, rule-making, and participation in a democratic society.

In seven community-led projects across the US—comprising disparate municipal sizes, jurisdiction types, and income and user groups served—self-organized developments by specialized nonprofits offer potent examples of how housing can be tailored to the unique needs of people and places and sustained over time. The projects include single-family homes on sovereign Oglala Lakota land in South Dakota, studios and tiny houses for formerly homeless people in Iowa City, San Diego, and Seattle, multigenerational live/work lofts for Hispanic makers and creative workers in Santa Fe, and duplexes and townhomes for farm workers in Southern California's Central Valley. The specificity of their designs for communities and their effectiveness at meeting the needs of ignored user groups should persuade policymakers, elected officials, and voters to expand grants and low-cost financing for projects to serve a huge unaddressed demand among those earning below a median income.

> To sensitively shape the design of projects, nonprofit developers often rely on architects with proven records with the planned housing types, enabling them to control costs by adapting existing models to sites and programs, spending on details and materials where they can have the largest impact. The developers frequently possess within their organizations expansive local knowledge from years of programming experience informed by evidence-based analysis of what works within their particular sector of the housing market. At times, they supplement this knowledge by

The units at Siler Yard are designed as attached townhouses with creative spaces on the ground floor.

coordinating community meetings and public events to gather insight from groups of potential users and to demonstrate demand within an area. The developments often require zoning variances, whose approval is aided by community support gained through engagement with neighbors, elected officials, government administrators, and interest groups.

In Santa Fe, New Mexico, Daniel Werwath, of nonprofit developer New Mexico Inter-Faith Housing, engaged in an unusually extensive community development process to construct Siler Yard Arts + Creativity Center, a recently completed 65-unit multigenerational live/work loft project sheltering 144 residents, including 41 children. Initiated by the nonprofit Creative Santa Fe in 2012 with community engagement supported by a $285,000 NEA Our Town grant, the project kicked off with a market survey, identification of potential development sites, and organization of culturally specific public events, such as custom car shows, to gather input from Hispanic and Native American nontraditional artists and makers.

According to Werwath, zoning limits and affordability regulations systematically suppress the housing supply in Santa Fe. Local zoning codes reserve more than half the land for single-family homes and mandate affordable housing in other areas, while a lack of financing throttles construction of affordable units. A rapid influx of retirees and pandemic migrants has left the city 11,000 units short of its needs. Hispanic families with multigenerational ties to the area are confronted by housing precarity, while

Stephen Zacks

The planted courtyard at Vistas del Puerto offers ample seating and programming for resident seniors.

even people with six-figure incomes struggle to find a place to live.

"It's wild," Werwath said. "The rate of displacement in Santa Fe is unlike anything that's ever happened to this community that's been through some successive waves of gentrification. It's particularly challenging because the people being displaced are, in some cases, 14th- and 15th-generation Hispanic families who have lived here since the late 1600s."

For the $19 million Siler Yard development, New Mexico Inter-Faith Housing acquired a publicly owned brownfield site from the city at no cost in an industrial district southwest of downtown, surrounded by auto shops, storage facilities, and public utilities. Santa Fe-based Atkin Olshin Schade Architects (recently absorbed by MASS

The courtyard in the center of KFA and Leong Leong's Ariadne Getty Foundation Senior Housing project provides gathering space for resident seniors.

Design Group) designed the project as attached townhomes based on community input about the needs of artists and makers. Creative space located on the ground level has cement floors, large contiguous walls to work on, outdoor storage and work areas, sound insulation, and northern and southern sun exposure. Dwelling units are on the second floor.

Like most affordable housing, the development demanded a complex series of funding sources, including $9.6 million from federal low-income tax credits, a $5.4 million Housing and Urban Development (HUD) mortgage at 3.2 percent interest, and $1.8 million from assorted charitable contributions, solar tax credits, and state affordable housing tax credits. Werwath applied three times for the federal tax credits before they were finally awarded, delaying the project for years. The eventual result was 100 percent income-restricted, net-zero-energy rentals running on 100 percent electricity and costing lessees from $420 to $1,200 a month.

In Long Beach, California, zoning for high-density development, access to publicly owned land, and public funding facilitated a project dedicated half to families, half to formerly homeless people.[2] Situated one block from the Metro A Line—a light-rail line from downtown Los Angeles to Long Beach, completed in 1990—the 47-unit Vistas del Puerto, designed by affordable housing specialists KFA, initially gained a density bonus due to its siting in a transit-oriented district. The project employs thoughtful space planning and generous open spaces to combine supportive studio housing for formerly homeless individuals and two- to three-bedroom units for individuals and families earning 30–50 percent of the area's median income. Bright-green planters, wood-plank balcony railings and benches, and furniture for groups to sit and gather outside accent courtyards for children to play, rooftop terraces, and a central stairway from the street that references Long Beach's shoreline cliffs. Street-level commercial space is designated for offices or community services, and on the interior, ground-level case management offices are staffed with supportive programs for residents.

2   More than 580,000 people were unsheltered in the US in 2020, according to the most recent HUD estimates.

John Arnold, a KFA partner, negotiated potential sensitivities around the relative bulk of the five-story mass by setting it against a commercial alleyway in the rear, stepping its street-facing facade down to three stories in front. "The biggest gesture at the front was that stairway that goes from the street up to the courtyard," Arnold said. "That was a way to really open up the project and engage the street, not be fearful of the street. It has an openness that matches the neighborhood. We were really evoking that beachy feeling of the steps going down to the beach."

Vistas del Puerto received financing from the city, low-income tax credits from the state and federal government, and rent supplemented by a California rent voucher similar to Section 8 that dedicates a fixed number of vouchers to buildings on a project basis in perpetuity. Since the project began, new California state laws further reversed restrictive zoning regulations, allowing greater building height and reducing parking requirements. Arnold thinks policymakers should also consider reducing mandatory unit sizes and open space requirements.

"A lot of cities going through growing pains have to let go of suburban ideals, which usually revolve around parking and open space," Arnold said. "On-site open space is difficult. The volume isn't as important as the quality of open space. Cities could let go of fear of heights and the fear that constituents are going to get mad and drive them out of office. Long Beach, in particular, has been supportive of bigger changes and is among the best in southern California that I've experienced."

Another KFA-designed development in the Los Angeles area produced 98 universally accessible studio and one- to two-bedroom apartments for LGBT seniors within a curving, five-story stucco volume in Hollywood. Drawing on the conceptual design for the LGBT Center's Anita May Rosenstein Campus by Leong Leong and expertise from for-profit developer Thomas Safran & Associates (TSA), which specializes in luxury and high-quality affordable housing, the Ariadne Getty Foundation Senior Housing contains supportive services and robust community space for LGBT seniors. Vistas del Puerto includes a lounge with a TV, pool table, and piano, a group kitchen, a gym, a planted courtyard with patio furniture, and a landscaped passage to the LGBT Center.

"The LGBT Center led the development of the programming," said KFA Senior Associate Monica Rodriguez, who managed the project. "The people at LGBT played a pretty strong role, and they were putting the program together and what they wanted in their building, and what the senior housing should have in terms of amenities. The design we took from our experience of working on affordable senior housing and some of the things that TSA likes to see in its buildings. They are one of the firms that really do pay attention to design."

Residents can obtain case management help, home meals, in-home care, benefits assistance, physical and mental health care, HIV support, counseling, support groups, and a huge number of monthly activities and events. The LGBT Center's campus also includes a four-story, 26-unit youth housing building and a 100-bed shelter for homeless youth.

The complex received funding from California's Tax Credit Allocation Committee (TCAC) program, which supplements federal low-income tax credits with capital from state bonds and property taxes to promote private investment in long-term affordable rental housing. Private investors, foundations, the City of Los Angeles, and LA County also provided funds. There are also project-based rent vouchers allocated to the building.

Along with the TCAC program and statewide density mandates, California has boosted development of affordable housing with a property tax exemption for three to five years after the purchase of land during the construction phase. In 2016, Los Angeles voters approved Proposition HHH, a $1.2 billion housing bond to fund up to 10,000 units of new permanent supportive housing and affordable housing over 10 years. California's 2018 No Place Like Home Act

BNIM's Ivy Senior Apartments fit 52 studio apartments for formerly unhoused seniors on a triangular infill site in San Diego.

One of Thunder Valley's 21 single-family homes, each of which is equipped with east-facing entrances and solar panels.

At Ivy Senior Apartments, circulation is facilitated by terraces that wrap around a central courtyard and provide direct access to private units.

also provided up to $2 billion from bonds for development of permanent low-barrier supportive housing for people with mental health needs who are experiencing homelessness. Low-barrier shelters make housing available with few requirements. They seek to keep unsheltered people housed regardless of rule violations, offering intensive services to mediate problems. Most recently, in November 2022, Angelinos passed a ballot measure dedicating 4 and 5.5 percent taxes on property sales of $5 million and $10 million or more, respectively, to fund aid for tenants and creation of affordable housing.

The Ivy Senior Apartments in San Diego is another permanently supportive project in California made possible by an increased density allowance and special funding sources. Designed by BNIM for seniors with chronic physical or mental health needs who have experienced homelessness, the project fits 52 studio apartments on a triangular infill site in the Clairmont Mesa East area. It belongs to a growing number of permanent supportive housing developments that adopt a "housing first" approach to homelessness, directly providing studio apartments to unsheltered people.

The developer, Wakeland Housing and Development Corporation, has built and manages more than 7,500 homes on 53 projects throughout the state. But after Wakeland bought the commercial property, it encountered opposition from the adjacent neighborhood. It engaged in extensive outreach to the city council and planning board and held public meetings to build trust with opponents, explaining how the project's supportive services would preclude many of the problems they anticipated. According to the Corporation for Supportive Housing, 90 percent of formerly homeless people who are offered permanently supportive housing remain housed after one year.

BNIM mediated opposition from community members in the low-lying surrounding neighborhood with a design that resembles a tech hub more than supportive housing for formerly unsheltered people. Its angled articulation of windows; mixture of green glass; white, muted green, and red-stripe-painted stucco; and aluminum-screened stairwell orient circulation and open space around a landscaped courtyard containing a community garden and seating, outdoor stairwells and balconies, and terraced entrances to private apartments outfitted with mini-kitchens and bathrooms.

The panoply of programs offered by Vistas del Puerto, like the LGBT Center and Ivy Senior Apartments, embodies a community vision of California's political constituency to offer public assistance and extensive financing sources to make supportive housing possible. Case workers and staff help residents acquire medical services and obtain financial assistance, gain social security, organize medical schedules, and provide transportation to appointments. The California Department of Health Care Services' (DHCS) Projects for Assistance in Transition from Homelessness (PATH) program supports community-based outreach, mental health and substance abuse treatment, and case management. DHCS's Program of All-Inclusive Care for the Elderly (PACE) also provides medical and social services to residents who would otherwise live in nursing homes.

With the injection of funds from property taxes in California and Los Angeles, according to Wakeland, supportive housing developments in the state are opening at a rate of one per week, as opposed to one per month previously. The project received financing and assistance from the San Diego Housing Commission, US Department of Housing and Urban Development HOME Fund, Housing Trust Fund, Inclusionary Affordable Housing Fund, City of San Diego, California Housing Finance Agency's Special Needs Housing Projects, Federal Home Loan Bank of San Francisco's Affordable Housing Program, California Community Reinvestment Corporation, and Wells Fargo's Community Lending and Investment.

Thunder Valley Community Development Corporation (CDC) built 23 single-family homes, designed by Pyatt Studio Architecture & Planning, on the Pine Ridge Oglala Lakota reservation in South Dakota. The design centers around a holistic vision of the Lakota people's connection to the land and its contribution to the tribe's ongoing work toward liberation. The project embodies a concept of regenerative community development that aims to support education in the Lakota language, food sovereignty, regional equity, social enterprise, workforce development, and youth leadership, along with housing and homeownership. The constraints came almost entirely from access to capital, however.

Thunder Valley CDC is a grassroots, indigenous-led nonprofit founded in 2007 by community members spurred to action during a traditional spiritual ceremony to solve the tribe's housing shortage. According to Kimberly Pelkofsky, director of development and planning, as many as 4,000 tribal members live in substandard housing, often in trailers or 20-person households overcrowded in two-bedroom homes. Mold and respiratory problems are common.

In 2011, the organization acquired 34 acres of deeded "fee-simple" land—privately owned land on the reservation, rather than land owned by the tribe or the federal government—to develop outside of the constrictions of tribal trust land administered by the Bureau of Indian Affairs, which imposes onerous financing requirements. Working with Rob Pyatt of Pyatt Studio, Thunder Valley CDC spent

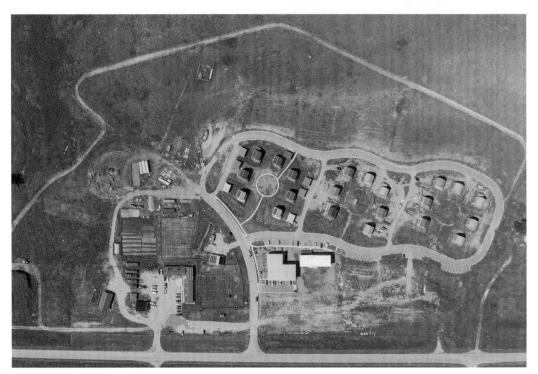

Thunder Valley's 21 single-family homes are arranged in three groups of seven around Lakota tipi circles.

For Neumann Monson Architects' Cross Park Place to be built, Iowa City created a new zoning category to accommodate 26 units and reduced parking requirements.

a year engaging the community in gatherings throughout the Pine Ridge reservation to develop a site plan and design for homes and common spaces rooted in Lakota lifeways. Twenty-one single-family homes with east-facing entrances and solar-paneled roofs are oriented in three groups of seven around tipi circles, shared as common spaces among homeowners. The development includes a three-acre demonstration farm; agricultural support buildings; a bunkhouse for artists, performers, and family members to sleep during tribal ceremonies; a community center for senior proms, bingo, trainings and workshops; playgrounds; and a school.

"It really is rooted in Lakota lifeways," says Pelkofsky. "It's not just some houses near a school; it really looks at what a Lakota community would be like if it was given a chance to flourish."

Instead of using federal funding, the project sought out private donations, grants, and loans. Two homes used a state tax credit program to support affordable housing. Some homeowners received loans through the US Department of Agriculture (USDA)'s Mutual Self-Help Housing program for low-income families to construct homes. Most of them received low-interest bank loans through a USDA rural development program or through a Veterans Administration-backed program. The three- and four-bedroom homes sell for $180,000 and $200,000, respectively, subsidized by Thunder Valley CDC.

In some cases, community-led housing developments originate in public agencies' requests for proposals to develop publicly owned sites, seeking to address critical shortages in an area's housing supply. The Rosaleda Village project began because the California High-Speed Rail planned to pass through the site of dedicated farmworker housing in Wasco, a center of almond and rose cultivation in California's heavily agricultural Central Valley region. The original farmworker dwellings had been situated within a barracks-like structure converted from a World War II POW camp. The new development relocates the workers' homes to a 17-acre site two miles away.

Southern California affordable housing specialists M.W. Steele designed Rosaleda Village as a neighborhood of 226 duplex townhouses and stacked apartments resembling the single-family homes of the surrounding area. A more condensed site plan would normally have been called for by the large scale of the multifamily development, but through workshops with the community, the architects responded to a desire for a style of living radically distinguished from the previous army encampment.

"That's kind of unique to this project," said Michael P. Paluso, architect and managing principal at M.W. Steele. "They're duplexes that are two-story units, so they're like townhomes. Typically, we wouldn't do that, but it's something that

Stephen Zacks

through the workshops with the community ahead of time was desirable."

The townhouse-style units and stacked apartments are spread out along blocks laid out like a suburban subdivision. The townhomes combine two duplex apartments under one peaked roof, with one accessible bedroom and bathroom on the ground floor and additional bedrooms and a bathroom on the second story. The stacked apartments are also contained within smaller volumes, unified by covered exterior staircases extending from slanted roofs.

The community workshops also emphasized the need for safe spaces for kids to play, which led to a site plan that incorporates shared playgrounds in open yards behind the homes, along with outdoor seating areas equipped with barbecues. Rosaleda Village also has a dedicated preschool operated by the Kern County public school system serving 144 children, as well as a community building for the neighborhood. A health clinic is planned on the remaining parcel.

The rail authority funded one-fifth of the development costs, alongside state financing and federal low-income tax credits. Paluso laments the slowness of the minimum two years it takes to develop most of these projects: "The waiting list for these affordable housing projects that we work on shows that there's a desperate need for them. There will be a 50-unit project, and the waiting list is 1,500-people deep. While there are different state, local, and federal policies that are trying to help bring about more affordable units, it's never going to be done quickly. It's a slow process."

In Iowa City, public agencies also played a leading role in the development of housing devoted to chronically unsheltered people. The local homeless coordinating board formed a stakeholder group to address the fact that a well-defined number of chronically homeless people in the community had an especially large number of high-intensity interactions with police officers, jails, hospitals, and ambulance and emergency services. The coordinating board—composed of representatives of the Iowa City Housing Authority, nonprofit housing developer Shelter House, substance abuse and mental health service providers, a jail alternative program, the local housing trust fund, and a police officer—conducted a four-and-a-half-year case study analyzing the public cost of social services to people experiencing chronic homelessness.

"We essentially made the case for permanent supportive housing by identifying the amount of money that was being expended, the nature of the services across the different systems for them to be cycling in no particular order through this circuit of high-cost services, only to recidivate back onto the streets of our community," said Shelter House Executive Director Crissy Canganelli.

Shelter House had earlier encountered community opposition to an emergency shelter it opened in 2010. The case eventually went to the Iowa Supreme Court, which ruled in its favor. But the experience changed the organization's approach to development. For Cross Park Place, a 26-unit apartment building with a charcoal brick and light-wood-slatted exterior designed by Iowa City-based Neumann Monson Architects and completed in 2019, Shelter House first gained support from the city, which helped create a new type of zoning category for long-term community housing. This allowed it to increase the residential use of the first floor and reduce parking requirements. During five years of fundraising, the organization built understanding and support within the community, demonstrating its intention to improve people's lives and improve systems while reducing the burden on jails and emergency and inpatient psychiatric care services.

Cross Park Place takes a "housing first" approach, directly providing permanent studio apartments to people who are unhoused. The goal is for residents to live at this low-barrier shelter with few questions or strings attached, despite a high frequency of narcotics abuse and mental illness among the intended residents. The architects used trauma-informed design to offer a noninstitutional environment, employing warm, natural-looking materials, daylit living room and kitchen areas, private bathrooms, and beds in secure-feeling nooks with built-in, dark-wood-patterned shelves and cabinets. "Really it's an apartment building," said Dan Broffitt, associate architect at Neumann Monson. "We went for residential feel as much as we could."

"The precedent had a design like a studio apartment," added Tim Schroeder, Neumann Monson principal and president. "It's all aimed at giving more of a sense of permanence and belonging to the person who's housed there. Having a keen sense of any stigma that could be attached to living in a facility like this and trying to design it to be durable but still pleasant."

Initially, Shelter House was unable to find a funding source to build apartments entirely dedicated to chronically homeless people. In 2016, the National Housing Trust Fund, established by Congress after the 2008 mortgage-backed securities crisis, finally began to distribute funding, enabling the project to begin development. Eventually, Shelter House supplemented these grants with commercial loans to complete the project, taking on the risk of private loans. The Iowa City Housing Authority provides special rental vouchers to the residents for operating revenues and expenses. The building is staffed with program managers, social workers, and nurse practitioners to mediate conflicts and connect residents with services.

The Tiny House Villages in Seattle exemplify how radical new approaches to housing can emerge from observing what's going on in a community. Among the most extensive community-led developments for people without shelter, the encampments of temporary homes are built and operated by nonprofit developer Low-Income Housing Institute (LIHI), which now runs 11 Tiny House Villages in Seattle and 19 in the Pacific Northwest region altogether— 900 tiny houses supporting more than 1,000 people annually. The aegis of the temporary shelters has an extraordinary backstory, involving the nonprofit, political leaders, building inspectors, corporate sponsors, and countless community groups.

The initiative grew out of the city's struggle to address homeless encampments in 2015. Unpermitted tent cities sponsored by multiple organizations, among them LIHI, populated many public spaces and private lots in Seattle. Reflecting a failure of housing affordability and the limits of the city's shelter infrastructure, they created unsafe conditions for unhoused people and were seen by many as eyesores, spurring public anxiety. A movement that advocated legalizing the tents was supported by the mayor at the time. The Seattle City Council reacted against them by seeking to have people who were squatting in tents arrested.

In response, LIHI worked with the mayor's office and a nearby church to sponsor a tent encampment on one of its developments to safely accommodate individuals, couples, families with children, and people with pets. It partnered with Nickelsville, a self-organized group within the camp, to coordinate and manage the site. In the cold, wet, windy conditions of Seattle winters, it was not enough, and LIHI sought a quick way to build safe and sturdy tiny houses with locked doors and privacy. Built by volunteers through the sponsorship of Home Depot, LIHI's first Tiny Houses were small sheds specifically dedicated to homeless veterans.

Sharon Lee, executive director of LIHI, negotiated with the city's Department of Construction and Inspection to expand the initiative and build the tiny houses on a larger scale. As long as they were temporary-use structures under 120 square feet, they fell outside of the building code and were permitted. Nonprofit community design center Environmental Works partnered with LIHI to develop site plans, situating the houses in neighborhood-like small groupings to encourage a sense of community among the residents.

"They've been helping us with the site plans," said Lee. "When we lay out a site, depending on how large, we want to create a sense of community. So if it's a larger site, we create a little neighborhood—a small grouping and then another small grouping—so it's not seen as 50 tiny houses all in a row.

A streetscape in one of the Low-Income Housing Institute's (LIHI) tiny house villages.

When we submit it to the building department, we present a site plan for permitting."

The units are 18-x-12-foot insulated structures on concrete skids with plywood walls, painted with colorful trim and supplied with electricity. Many come with accessible ramps. They cost $4,000 each for materials, built by a battalion of volunteers, block clubs, churches, and community organizations six days a week in a factory in Seattle or as group initiatives. Every village provides a large community kitchen, a laundry facility, private showers and bathrooms, staff offices, and other community spaces, with a cedar fence around its border. Within each village, case managers work out of offices in a few dedicated tiny houses to move people quickly into more permanent subsidized or private-market housing—ideally within six months. Each development has a community advisory committee composed of local businesses, council members, church representatives, neighbors, and service agencies that meet monthly to evaluate needs and offer support.

The engagement of local community leaders and elected officials, along with effective management of the shelters through design, planning, and provision of adequate facilities and social services, has mediated the opposition of neighbors common in temporary housing, according to Lee. "With the first two Tiny House Villages, we got serious opposition, because we like being in prime locations," Lee said. "We don't want to be in some dumpy industrial area. We're in every single city council district in Seattle, multifamily neighborhoods, residential neighborhoods, mixed-use neighborhoods...it's been great."

Increasingly, commentators, advocates, and policymakers blame restrictive zoning regulations that limit developments to single-family homes and prohibit multifamily apartment buildings, suggesting that the market will magically produce adequate supply without these restrictions. All other things being equal, many community-led developers and architects specializing in multifamily dwellings agree that restrictive zoning plays a significant role in limiting housing supply in many places. But limited access to capital for construction and funding for supportive services constitutes a huge under-acknowledged factor in reduced production.

Interviews with a dozen architects and developers of exemplary community-led developments for disparate scales and types of small towns, cities, and counties across the US suggest that housing developments that increase neighborhood density can be sensitively designed to improve the quality and scale of affordable and supportive housing for constituencies poorly served by the private real estate market, without causing a negative reaction among neighbors and voters. These examples emphatically indicate that community-led design and development processes can be broadly expanded to meet the needs of individuals and families earning less than the median income without resulting in the undesirable conditions of neglect and failure that led to the abandonment of the public housing model in the 1970s.

At the same time, we should not ignore the extent to which many of these affordable housing types require robust additional sources of capital and publicly funded supportive services to ensure that those earning below the median income—as well as people experiencing mental illnesses, drug dependency, and the need for other health and social services—can gain housing stability. The totality of these cases argue for a definition of what constitutes designing, developing, and policymaking for communities as not only the process of consultation, meeting, gathering input, and designing projects and policies around the desires of a given group, but also ensuring the provision of financing and supportive services to guarantee that a sufficient quantity and quality of housing is produced and that it is adequately managed over time for the particular needs of the constituents being served.

Community-Led Development Projects
Communal Space Floorplans

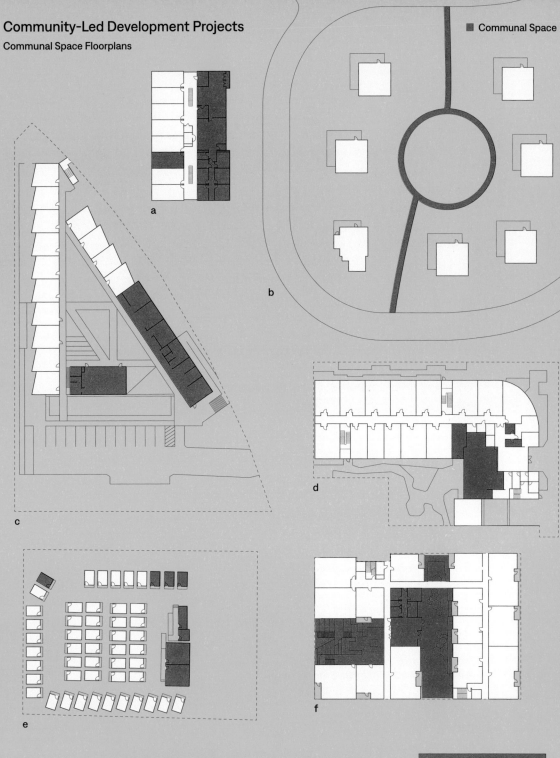

■ Communal Space

a   Cross Park Place, Neumann Monson Architects, Iowa City, IA
b   Thunder Valley CDC, Ferguson Pyatt Architects, Hoxie
     Collective, with Hubbard Studio, Porcupine, SD
c   Ivy Senior Apartments, BNIM, San Diego, CA
d   Ariadne Getty Foundation Senior Housing, KFA and Leong
     Leong, Los Angeles, CA
e   Tiny House Villages, Environmental Works Community Design
     Center, Seattle, WA
f   Vistas del Puerto, KFA, Los Angeles, CA
g   Siler Yard: Arts + Creativity Center, AOS, Santa Fe, NM

Finally Single (Room Occupancy)

Love is hard to find; good roommates harder still. And yet, for too long
there have been few alternatives to high-priced studio or one-bedroom
apartments. One solution is the single-room occupancy (SRO) dwelling.
SROs, which typically lack a kitchen, living space, or private bathroom, were
widely outlawed in the 20th century for health, safety, and maintenance
reasons. Today, however, SROs are on the rise. No longer boarding houses—
and no longer sponsored, as they once were, by the YMCA—SROs today take the form of university housing, co-living, and hostels.[i] Treehouse
Hollywood, designed by Soler Architecture and Knibb Design in Los Angeles,
targets young professionals, providing rooms for 60 residents across
three- and five-bedroom and studio units. These co-living units are minimal: they include only ensuite bathrooms and outsource cooking, living,
eating, socializing, and working spaces to other locations in the complex.
Another co-living venture, The Outpost, designed by Beebe Skidmore
in Portland, Oregon, takes shape as a twisted boxy form built upon an existing single-family home. Inside, 16 rooms negotiate the rotating plan
geometry, somehow sandwiching in a second floor of dedicated communal
space. Although the name signifies being on the cutting edge of a new
movement, its structure refers to the surrounding homes, which are traditional in style. The exterior character reinforces this dual concept,
with rotations in cladding and frontages but similarity in color choice and
materiality—establishing a nuanced vision of collective living in solo
structures. In nearby Portland, Jolene's First Cousin—a mixed-use, low-rise
SRO scheme—provides 11 rooms for people transitioning away from
homelessness. Furnished only with a small storage area, a bed, and a sink,
the rooms stack on top of communal bathroom, kitchen, living, and dining spaces. Compared to units in traditional apartment buildings, units in
SROs can be smaller and more nimble, often untethered by wet walls
or plumbing stacks. By departing from the typical model of thinking only
in a fixed-unit framework, SROs move towards one based upon people,
and the diverse ways in which we can provide them housing—together, and
alone again.

---

i   Recently, the Minneapolis City Council enacted an ordinance aimed squarely at bringing SROs back.
     Minneapolis Planning Commission Member Keith Ford noted, "My time on the City Council, 50
     years ago now, we were dealing with getting rid of SROs...[where now we are bringing them back] to
     provide for a well-regulated and well-operated SRO system." See "In a Bid to Offer More Affordable
     Housing Options, Minneapolis Council Members Propose Bringing Back the Rooming House,"
     https://www.minnpost.com/metro/2021/07/in-a-bid-to-offer-more-affordable-housing-options
     -minneapolis-council-members-propose-bringing-back-the-rooming-house/.

Split Plans

Ground floor

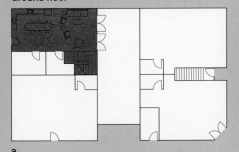

Second level

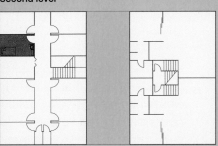

a

Second level

Third level

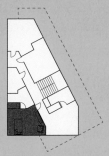

b

Third level

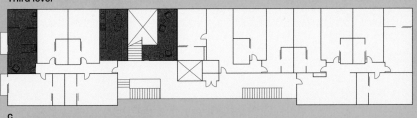

c

a   Jolene's First Cousin, Brett Schulz Architect, Portland, OR
b   The Outpost, Beebe Skidmore, Portland, OR
c   Treehouse Hollywood, Soler Architecture & Knibb Design, Los Angeles, CA

Marginalia

Solar panels, electric-car charging stations, geothermal wells, mini-splits, heat pumps, smart switches/lights/panels/devices, tankless water heaters, battery storage walls, overhangs for summer solar shading: these are but a few of the relatively new elements that architects increasingly opt to creatively incorporate into their buildings to make them more resilient. These kinds of elements appeared often in the projects we surveyed and seemed integral to this book's broader themes. When it comes to resiliency, we might also include more native plants, better floodproofing, raised ground floors, and large indoor bike parking rooms (soon to be more fire-resistant for e-bikes and scooters). Other *au courant* elements were off-the-shelf truss systems, pre-engineered walls, integrated weather barrier sheathing, and many modes of modular offsite assembly, including a variety of pre-built A-frame cabins. Accessible details result in more step-free entryways, d-pulls for cabinets, door levers, and height-adjustable counters, cabinets, and desks. We might add that housing has become more colorful, with higher contrast, brighter exterior paints, more Hardie board, variation in planes, a lack of verticality, homogenous facades, random siding, sans-serif address numbers, casement windows, and the color gray. On the interiors, we heard rumors of more floating shelves in kitchens, open floor plans, open kitchens, open homes, inclusion of a community room, extra space for remote work, more natural light, larger continuous spaces, fewer foyers, lower furniture, more bathrooms, five-inch baseboards, one-piece shower pans, in-law suites, dual-color casework, more amenities, guest units for rent, micro-units, large tiles, storage built into closets, subway tile, birch wood, and white walls.

a   Off-the-Shelf Truss
b   Height-Adjustable Desk
c   Accessible Shower
d   Integrated Weather Barrier Sheathing
e   Mini-Split
f   Sans-Serif Address Numbers
g   Drawer D-Pull
h   Solar Panels
i   Five-Inch Baseboard
j   Casement Windows
k   Door Lever
l   Subway Tile
m   Native Plants
n   Electric-Car Charging Station

Small and Skinny

There exists big value in building small. Whereas the market pushes both suburban homes and multifamily housing to grow only larger in scale, we have identified many skinny homes, townhomes, odd lots, and small urban infill projects that disregard these norms. In response to exorbitant land costs in some markets, developers are increasingly turning to oddly shaped, narrow, or otherwise undesirable lots and challenging designers to maximize their livability. One immediate benefit of designing on smaller lots is that it creates more attainable rental and homeownership opportunities from sheer smallness. While the average home has grown over the past few decades, the typical household has shrunk,[i] creating an inverse reality in US cities, whereby those with less money must pay to live in homes that are larger than necessary. Finally, small homes—especially those with common walls, such as townhomes—use less energy than large, detached dwellings. These projects, which weave a common thread of less-is-more, show that typical zoning and regulatory standards do not meet the moment. Less space and less energy use at a better price point is often preferred but not provided.[ii]

For both overlooked urban lots and underused suburban parcels, small and skinny designs have offered alternatives to vacant lots. Some city agencies have partnered with architects to generate ideas for small lots that developers typically overlook. In 2021, Only If Architecture completed work on its Narrow House project, originally a finalist in the "Big Ideas for Small Lots NYC" competition jointly run by New York's Department of Housing Preservation and Development and the American Institute of Architects. Other notable projects of the type in recent years include the Black Street Development by Module, Habitat for Humanity's Oxford Green by ISA, and the Pittsfield Tyler Street Development by Utile. All imagine new typologies that both reference their historic context and anticipate a denser urbanism in the future—designing smaller spaces for the long haul. In her essay, Inga Saffron examines the rowhouse through both personal and architectural dimensions, focusing on one of the nation's meccas of the skinny typology: Philadelphia.

i "Whatever Happened to the Starter Home?" The *New York Times*, https://www.nytimes.com/2022/09/25/upshot/starter-home-prices.html.
ii "What Happened When Minneapolis Ended Single-Family Zoning," Bloomberg, https://www.bloomberg.com/opinion/articles/2022-08-20/what-happened-when-minneapolis-ended-single-family-zoning?leadSource=uverify%20wall.

by Inga Saffron

My Philadelphia rowhouse began its life shortly after the Civil War. It was originally three rooms stacked vertically like children's blocks, with a cooking area and privy located in the yard. Such tiny houses are known as "Trinities" in Philadelphia, and they were built as cheap shelter for immigrants and the working class. Because Trinities were often purchased on an installment plan, their owners could expand their properties as their circumstances improved, a practice that Jane Jacobs dubbed "unslumming." My Trinity was probably enlarged in the early twentieth century when an addition was put on the back, creating a second room on each floor. The owners no doubt used the occasion to install indoor plumbing and gas heating. In the 1980s, a loft-like fourth story was added. Today, the former Trinity is a four-bedroom, two-bath house, the vertical equivalent of a modest rancher. Yet, the entire property, which includes a cozy, tree-shaded patio, could probably fit within the confines of a typical suburban driveway.

If you were to look out from one of Philadelphia's downtown skyscrapers, you would see block after block of similar red-brick rowhouses, stretching for miles across the pancake-flat landscape, some 400,000 in all. Philadelphia certainly didn't invent the form, but it has embraced the row like no other American city. Attached houses, which are typically 16 to 20 feet wide in Philadelphia, account for about 60 percent of the city's housing stock.[1] They come in a variety of sizes, with the Trinity being merely the starter version. The larger rowhouses are sometimes jokingly called Quaker mansions because their facades are so plain. There are also ornate Victorian examples, dripping with gables and gingerbread and clocking in at 4,000 square feet. But whether they are glorified tenements or miniature palaces, all rowhouses share party walls with their neighbors. This intimacy sets the pattern for our daily lives: how we move through the streets, how we socialize, how we arrange our civic relations. People of all classes and races live in rowhouses. That makes the rowhouse the city's most democratic residential form.

1   "Philadelphia, PA, Housing Statistics," Infoplease, https://www.infoplease.com/us/census/pennsylvania/philadelphia/housing-statistics.

Philadelphia takes pride in being a city of homes—single-family homes, to be technical about it. Yet it remains one of the densest, and most affordable, big cities in America. How can that be? From everything we've been told about America's growing housing crisis, single-family zoning is the enemy of affordability. If we hope to create enough housing for everyone, advocates say, we must build more apartment buildings, more microunits, more ADUs, more SROs. They are not wrong. But they also tend to underestimate the

Philadelphia's ubiquitous rowhouse typology may offer solutions for a growing housing density issue.

An aerial view shows blocks in Philadelphia lined with rowhouses.

potential of the humble rowhouse. Packed together on small lots, these compact homes can yield densities that rival some apartment buildings. The rowhouse can make our communities more affordable, sustainable, and walkable. There's another word I would add to that list, one that has been less in vogue these days: neighborly.

> The social changes brought on by the pandemic are likely to only increase the appeal of the rowhouse. Now that more people are able to work remotely, they can, theoretically, live anywhere. Although many professionals have decamped for the suburbs, others have discovered that the supply of moderately priced houses and starter homes is actually quite limited, especially in inner-ring communities. As a result, many young families are forced to choose between living in the exurbs or remaining in a cramped city apartment. For low-income workers, there are even fewer options for decent housing.

This is where the rowhouse can offer a middle ground. With a rowhouse, you get the privacy of a single-family home, along with access to a yard, but generally at a lower price point. It's spacious enough to set up a home office or makeshift classroom and accommodate a washer-dryer. Yet, it's environmentally superior to a free-standing house. Its compact form and shared party walls mean a rowhouse requires much less energy to heat and cool.

> Philadelphia's dense rowhouse districts are also the model for the sustainable 15-minute neighborhood that is now the subject of so much buzz. The city's rowhouse neighborhoods are typically arranged around a commercial street lined with stores, restaurants, and, maybe, an elementary school, which means you don't need to get in a car for your basic needs. After I began working from home during the pandemic, I was surprised to discover the busy weekday world outside my front door: The steady parade of people walking dogs. Daycare workers marching their charges to the playground. The chatty USPS delivery guy who wanted to talk about my columns in the *Philadelphia Inquirer.* In the evenings, my neighbors drank "Quarantinis" on their front steps, and we toasted each other from our socially distanced perches. I actually felt more connected during those early, scary months of 2020 than ever before.

Of course, rowhouse neighborhoods aren't unique to cities. Plenty of suburban communities have welcomed townhouse developments into the mix. Compared with stand-alone houses that sit on half-acre lots, these developments can be quite dense. But they have nothing on the traditional Philadelphia rowhouse block. Thanks to the preponderance of tightly packed rowhouses, Philadelphia has the smallest average lot size of any American city: 1,100 square feet. My four-bedroom house occupies just

Inga Saffron

980 square feet of the Earth, garden included. That works out to about 40 houses to the acre. Philadelphia may not be as dense as New York, but it's virtually tied for density with Chicago and Miami—two cities known for high-rise living.[2]

2   "The 300 Largest Cities in the United States by Population 2023," World Population Review, https://worldpopulationreview.com/us-cities.

3   "Vehicle Ownership in U.S. Cities Data and Map," Governing, https://www.governing.com/archive/car-ownership-numbers-of-vehicles-by-city-map.html.

Suburban townhouse developments rarely achieve Philadelphia-level densities for one obvious reason: parking. The space allotted for streets and grass also tends to be more generous. Once you make room for those amenities, you're lucky to get 18 houses to the acre. Because Philadelphia has remained faithful to its Colonial-era grid, residential streets in its older neighborhoods are rarely wider than 35 feet, and some are just 10 feet across. More important, most rowhouses built before the 1950s have no dedicated parking. Although Philadelphians are just as obsessed with their cars as other Americans, they have learned to make do with street parking. A third of the city's households still don't own cars.[3] The concentration of rowhouses is what allows Philadelphia to sustain one of the most extensive transit systems in the country.

Still, today's rowhouse is not Ben Franklin's rowhouse. During the late twentieth century, when Philadelphia's economy was in decline, almost no new housing was built. The market began to revive in the early 2000s, after the city introduced a generous property tax abatement aimed at encouraging the middle class to buy homes in the city. Construction has pretty much been nonstop since then. Tens of thousands of new rowhouses (as well as thousands of apartment units) have been built across the city, and many more have been renovated. Since most new construction is infill, and replaces buildings that were lost during the long decline, the new houses are simply fitted into the empty space. But although the modern rowhouse occupies the same footprint as its predecessors, it has been aggressively adapting to modern tastes and technology.

It's safe to say that no one is building Trinities in Philadelphia anymore. Most new rowhouses are now four stories, 3,000 square feet, and squarely aimed at middle-class professionals, with prices often exceeding $400,000. (By contrast, my expanded Trinity is still less than 2,000 square feet.) We've also seen the rise of a new luxury format that I call the McRowhouse, five stories and more than 5,000 square feet. One way to fit all that square footage on the same rowhouse lot is to build up—one reason the average rowhouse has gotten significantly taller in recent years. A cluster of 65-foot-high McRowhouses just went up in my neighborhood, with prices starting at $2 million. Elevators are now standard in such developments. I've toured McRowhouses that come with media rooms and rooftop dog parks. But even the 3,000-square-foot versions boast amenities that

ISA's Tiny Tower origami staircase doubles as a circulation core and light well.

The 1,250 square foot single-family home glows at each of its five levels. While mindful of setbacks, it fills the site boundaries to achieve an elegant but efficient form.

Inga Saffron

Oxford Green's facade module pays contextual tribute within an economy of means, addressing both scale and cadence as critical means of creating human-scaled neighborhoods.

are considered standard in the suburbs, including kitchen islands, home offices, 10-foot ceilings, and, increasingly, dedicated parking.

When Philadelphia overhauled its zoning code a decade ago, it briefly toyed with the idea of prohibiting parking in all new rowhouses. In the end, the city decided to leave the decision up to the developer. And since off-street parking is a highly desired amenity, virtually all new rowhouses today come with a dedicated parking spot of some kind. But Philadelphia planners did manage to insert a clause in the new code that prohibits garages that front onto residential streets. Today's garages are usually tucked in the back of the rowhouse and accessed through a common driveway or alley street. The arrangement works particularly well when the developer controls a large site and can arrange two rows of houses around an internal courtyard. Besides providing access to the garages, the drive aisle often doubles as a communal play space or a venue for cookouts and neighborly get-togethers. Since the driveways are collectively maintained, they effectively force residents to work together as a community to keep them in good shape.

As new rowhouses have gotten bigger, so have old ones. Across the city, owners are adding an extra floor to their nineteenth-century rowhouses. These overbuilds are primarily concentrated in neighborhoods populated by affluent professionals. In the past, this demographic might have headed for the suburbs once they started a family. Being able to add another bedroom or two to a 1,400-square-foot house makes it easier to raise children in the city. Planners are deeply torn over the trend. They want middle-class families to put down roots and pay taxes. But the overbuilds can transform former working-class houses into luxury properties that can easily sell for $1 million.

4   "Philadelphia Housing Market," Redfin, https://www.redfin.com/city/15502/PA/Philadelphia/housing-market.
5   "QuickFacts: Philadelphia City, Pennsylvania," United States Census Bureau, https://www.census.gov/quickfacts/philadelphiacity-pennsylvania.

Overall, Philadelphia remains one of most affordable big cities in the US. You can still buy a decent-sized rowhouse for under $250,000, according to Redfin.[4] That price is actually less than what it costs to build a new home these days. Philadelphia still has patches of abandonment, where you can find a vacant shell for under $80,000. But planners worry the city won't stay a bargain much longer. Philadelphia is a conundrum: It has the highest home ownership rate among Northeastern cities, 53 percent. Yet it remains the poorest of America's 10 largest cities, with a poverty rate hovering around 22 percent.[5] Surprisingly, many poor families own their homes, thanks to a tradition of passing down Trinities to children and grandchildren. But that doesn't make those residents immune to displacement.

As in other cities, the grinding process of neighborhood change is transforming many old rowhouse neighborhoods. Over the past two decades, Graduate Hospital, a formerly Black neighborhood on the edge of Center City (downtown),

6   "Searching for a NewIdentity, Philadelphia's Most Gentrified Neighborhood Looks to Its African American Past," *Philadelphia Inquirer*, https://www.inquirer.com/philly/columnists/inga_saffron/philadelphia-neighborhood-names-graduate-hospital-marian-anderson-20180719.html.

has grown dramatically more affluent and more white.[6] Now, the same thing is happening in the next neighborhood over, Point Breeze. Of course, gentrification here, as elsewhere, is a many-layered story. Until the '80s, South Philadelphia's rowhouse neighborhoods were almost exclusively occupied by Italian, Irish, and Jewish families. Today, the area is dominated by immigrants from Southeast Asia (Vietnamese, Cambodian, Burmese, Bhutanese, Karen, Chin) and Latin America (Mexican, primarily). One section has even been nicknamed (not very accurately) Little Saigon. We're also seeing an influx of young professionals in blue-collar enclaves like Fishtown, once the domain of construction workers, cops, and firefighters. What's remarkable is that the Philadelphia rowhouse continues to accommodate these shifting demographics generation after generation.

A few architects and developers have been pushing back against the notion that a bigger rowhouse is a better rowhouse. In 2018, ISA, an architecture firm run by Brian Phillips and Deb Katz, got a lot of attention for building a 12-foot-wide rowhouse on a 29-foot-deep lot, which they named "Tiny Tower."[7] Somehow they managed to pack 1,250 square feet into five, light-filled levels (plus a roof deck). In its disciplined use of space, the house resembles something you might find in Japan. Every surface, including a custom-fabricated steel staircase that unwinds like origami, is painted white. Furnishings are kept minimal. For the moment, the house stands alone on a block of similarly sized vacant lots. Unfortunately, all of them are still used by their owners for parking.

7   "Tiny Tower," ISA, https://www.is-architects.com/tiny-tower/op7gxqnf8zypje36ef72y2pckzdcz9.
8   "NOVO," Atrium Design Group, http://www.atriumdesigngroup.com/portfolio/novo/.

At the other end of the spectrum, Atrium Design Group recently completed a cluster of 5,000-square-foot houses on Wood Street, just north of the elegant Benjamin Franklin Parkway. Founded by architect-developer Shimi Zakin, Atrium specializes in McRowhouses. The facades of his Wood Street development, which is called NOVO, boast a luscious buff brick and are accented with rippled metal screens.[8] Inside, every surface has been slathered in fine wood and stone. Like most new rowhouses, the ground floor is dedicated primarily to housing cars. NOVO's two-car garages, which are accessed through a shared driveway, would look right at home in a high-end suburb. One advantage of putting the living areas on the upper floors is that the rooms are drenched in natural light. But what's most interesting about the design is that Zakin carved out a "mother-in-law" suite in the house's English-style basement, complete with a full kitchen and bath. One can imagine it being rented out some day as an apartment.

Those of us who live in older rowhouses have more modest aspirations. Because the working-class rowhouse is simply a vertical stack of rooms, it generally lacks the graces of more refined housing. Most Trinities have no entrance foyer, which means there is no mediating ground to transition from the public realm of the street into the private space of the house. Since the living room is usually located in the front, facing the street, visitors practically bump into the sofa the minute they walk in the door. There is no place to remove your shoes, hang your coat, or sign off on a package delivery. Although larger rowhouses from the late nineteenth century sometimes have small vestibules, those entrances rarely include a coat closet.

When I renovated my 16-foot-wide house a few years ago, one of my objectives was to create a more gracious entry sequence. The architects, Loomis MacAfee, solved the problem by moving the kitchen to the front of the house.[9] That allowed them to carve out a three-by-eight-foot vestibule at the entrance. A built-in, floor-to-ceiling cabinet separates the two spaces, providing the coat closet I've always wanted.

9   Loomis McAfee Architects, https://loomismcafee.com/?posts.

I've seen similarly inventive solutions around the city. Because there is so little room to waste in a 16-foot-wide rowhouse, most were built with "winders," tightly curved staircases that require the balance skills of a mountain goat to navigate. As rowhouse ceilings have gotten higher in new construction, architects have been able to design staircases with gentler ascents. Some Philadelphia architects have also been experimenting with double-height living rooms and mezzanines to make their houses feel airier. Even in those rare instances when the ground floor is not used for parking, some architects are now placing the kitchen and living room on the second floor. The first floor can be used as a home office or den, creating a nice transition between the street and the family spaces.

When it comes to energy efficiency, rowhouses are hard to beat. Huddled together, and sharing party walls, they keep each other warm. In the summer, the front and back windows provide cross-ventilation. Modern insulation and construction techniques allow designers to trim energy usage even more. The tradeoff is that some of the new, energy-efficient building skins, such as metal panels, look jarring next to an old brick-and-stone rowhouse. Since some developers don't involve architects in the construction process, many rowhouse facades are little more than an assortment of colored panels randomly arranged around the windows. These insulated houses may save energy in the short term, but I suspect it won't be long before they need to be reskinned. I've already seen one luxury development where the panels and flashings failed, water seeped inside, and the entire exterior had to be replaced. I'll take my 150-year-old brick Trinity any day.

In Austin, Texas, Habitat for Humanity is investing in building higher-density housing through the rowhouse model. Mueller Row Homes, designed by Michael Hsu Architects, gives a dynamic massing and elevation movement to the traditionally staccato housing type.

Utile's modular housing model takes on infill housing as a repeatable and scalable model for a variety of site conditions.

Designed by Only If Architecture in Brooklyn, Narrow House is a single-family home occupying a site that is only 13 feet, 4 inches wide.

The Philadelphia rowhouse has survived, in large measure, because of its adaptability and efficiency. A simple rectangular box, punctuated by windows, the rowhouse can be gutted, rebuilt, and turned into exactly the house you want. And then you can remake it all over again. As Philadelphia's historic preservationists like to say, the most environmentally friendly house is one that already exists. If you recoat the roof and patch the mortar every few years, a rowhouse will pretty much last forever.

When you think about it, the Philadelphia Trinity is a lot like the houses built by residents in the world's informal settlements. Those structures usually start out as one or two rooms. They're expanded as the owner's family and income grow. In a 2014 TED talk, the San Diego-based architect Teddy Cruz suggested that such an iterative approach could become a model for affordable housing in the US.[10] Of course, many favela residents do their own construction, something that is unlikely to happen widely in the US. But what if developers offered starter Trinities on lots that allowed for expansion? We know that many single-family communities in America are deeply resistant to apartment buildings. Perhaps the rowhouse, which is also a form of single-family housing, would be an easier sell?

So much of the national conversation around housing and climate change has focused on getting people to accept smaller living quarters. Housing advocates tend to get most excited about the boutique solutions—the microunits and ADUs. But we shouldn't dismiss the real yearning of ordinary Americans for a place of their own, a patch of yard, and a community of neighbors. Because it offers both privacy and affordability, the rowhouse is an attractive option. It won't solve all of America's housing needs, but the rowhouse might be the best hope we have to convince large numbers of people that they can live both sustainably and comfortably in cities.

10   "The Informal as Inspiration for Rethinking Urban Spaces: Architect Teddy Cruz Shares 5 Projects," TED Blog, https://blog.ted.com/architect-teddy-cruz-shares-5-projects/.

Small and Skinny Projects

Typical Floor Plans

Rowhouse

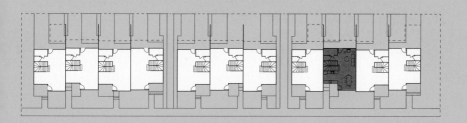

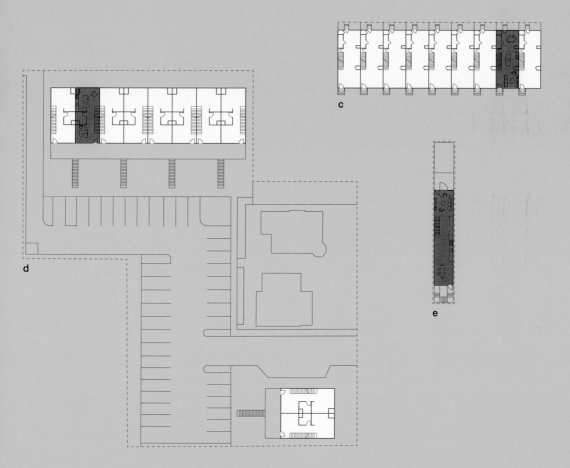

a

b

c

d

e

a   Habitat Mueller Row Homes, Michael Hsu Office of Architecture, Austin TX
b   Tiny Tower, ISA, Philadelphia, PA
c   Oxford Green, ISA, Philadelphia, PA
d   Pittsfield Tyler Street Development, Utile, Pittsfield, MA
e   Narrow House, Only If, Brooklyn, NY

Project Index

Map of Indexed Projects

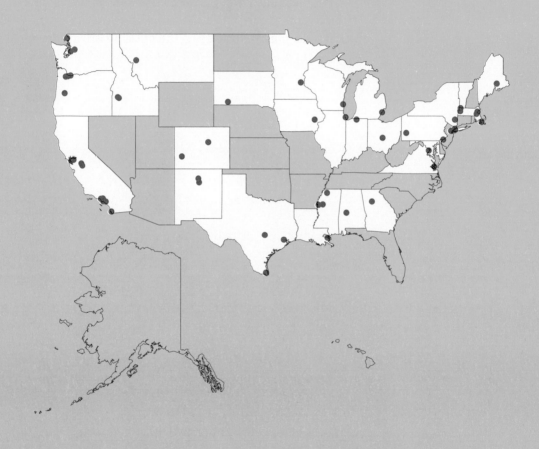

Afterword
by Farshid Moussavi

In the United States, and in many other parts of the world, we are facing a housing crisis. There is too little housing, and the housing we have is un-affordable for far too many. Developers are blamed for building housing for maximum profit, while governments are blamed for investing too little in building affordable housing, as well as their restrictive policies. But the projects compiled in this report by the Joint Center for Housing Studies demonstrate how designers can take a proactive approach to the crisis. Despite having to work within existing constraints, they exemplify the many roles that architecture can play in addressing the crisis we are confronting.

Three broad categories emerge from this work. First, there are projects that deal with the question of what kind of housing we should build. This includes projects that envision housing as a common resource; projects that house both families and solo occupants; projects with community-serving amenities; and emergency housing projects for those that require immediate shelter. Second, there are projects that ask how we should build housing. This category includes projects that propose to renovate and adapt existing buildings for housing to avoid demolition and deliver homes in a more affordable way; 3D-printed houses to build housing faster and in a more economical way; self-built houses that reduce construction costs; and houses that use modular, panelized, and premade components. Also in this category are projects that innovate on the financing side by, for example, collecting capital through crowdsourcing. The third category of projects compiled in this report asks how housing can be better connected to what surrounds it, from its immediate environment to the wider planet. The projects in this category include large-scale developments that create context; infill projects that artfully blend into their surroundings; projects that are designed to reduce energy usage; and projects that employ onsite water usage and retention and other sustainable water-management techniques to help individuals and households adapt to climate change.

Looking ahead, what can designers do to ensure that the houses we inhabit better suit our contemporary needs? In the twenty-first century, two significant issues that must be at the forefront of any housing project are equality and well-being (of individuals and the planet).

Equality is about offering people a choice of homes so that people with diverse living situations can find options that are suited to them. It is also about ensuring that housing is integrated and enables lower- and higher-income groups to live in proximity, thus fostering social inclusion. Equality is also about allowing different types of work to be carried out at home and enabling parents with young children to work from home should they need to.

When it comes to well-being, we need to consider the inclusion of green outdoor spaces (both for private and communal use), as well as the provision of spaces that nurture community-building to mitigate loneliness, or the provision of spaces for exercise and relaxation. Well-being is also related to empowering inhabitants to reconfigure their homes, should their circumstances change. This requires that we build flexibility into apartments right from the outset. Well-being is also related to what our home allows us to do in it. This means considering what we do at home now, compared to before the pandemic, and how our homes have to change to accommodate these activities. The well-being of individuals is intertwined with that of the planet, too. The reduction of energy, as well as carbon consumption, by the housing sector is a vital way to address planetary well-being. This is where co-living—in which inhabitants share spaces and resources—can offer a way to address this challenge.

One standard which is not often assessed in housing is 'pleasure' and 'enjoyment of living in a place', which are topics that can easily remain unspoken of in housing developments. We can learn much from France, which has a history of building social housing that, to this day, remains inspirational to its inhabitants. In order to deliver sufficient numbers of homes, the state builds social housing but also partners with the private sector to deliver market-rate housing in which the pleasure of living is of foremost importance. Such public-private partnerships allow the French state to take an active role in shaping privately led development proposals to that end.

Ultimately, what architects can do is highly influenced by how projects are procured and the space they are given for creativity. We need to keep being imaginative with procurement routes so that architects can generate spaces for living that allow people to dream. Where else would we dream, if not in our homes?

Contributors

Corinna Anderson is the publications coordinator at Harvard University's Joint Center for Housing Studies. She manages production of working papers, blogs, and other research and supports other communications projects at the Center.

Nate Berg is a staff writer for Fast Company magazine, covering design. His work has appeared in *The New York Times*, *The Atlantic*, *The Guardian*, *Wired*, *Curbed*, *National Public Radio*, and *99% Invisible*, among many others. He is based in Detroit.

Natalie Boverman is a dual Master in Urban Planning and Master in Architecture candidate at Harvard University's Graduate School of Design and a research assistant at the Joint Center for Housing Studies. Her work focuses on linking design at different scales, incremental development, timber, and rurality.

Yona Chung is an architect, urban designer, and thinker and a first-year Doctor of Design student at Harvard University's Graduate School of Design. Her research lies in the redevelopment of modern housing superblocks in East Asia to address the idea of resiliency and flexibility in today's anthropocentric climate.

Marianela D'Aprile is a writer and the deputy editor of *The New York Review of Architecture*. Her work has appeared in *The Nation*, *Jacobin*, *Metropolis*, and *The Architectural Review*, among others.

Daniel D'Oca is an urban planner and Associate Professor in Practice of Urban Planning at Harvard University's Graduate School of Design and a principal and cofounder of the New York-based architecture, urban design, and planning firm Interboro Partners.

Chris Herbert is the managing director at Harvard University's Joint Center for Housing Studies and a lecturer in the Department of Urban Planning and Design at Harvard's Graduate School of Design.

Emily Hsee is a Master in Architecture candidate at Harvard University's Graduate School of Design and a research assistant at the Joint Center for Housing Studies.

Farshid Moussavi is an internationally acclaimed architect and Professor in Practice of Architecture at Harvard University's Graduate School of Design.

Sam Naylor is a practicing architect in Boston, where he focuses on housing at multiple scales, and a researcher studying cooperative design around the world.

Adele Peters is a senior writer at *Fast Company* magazine who focuses on solutions to some of the world's largest problems, from climate change to homelessness. She is a two-time winner of the SEAL Award for Environmental Journalism. Previously, she worked with GOOD, Biolite, and the Sustainable Products and Solutions program at UC Berkeley.

Inga Saffron is a Pulitzer Prize-winning architecture critic for *The Philadelphia Inquirer*.

Lilly Saniel-Banrey is a designer of all sorts of things. She is interested in the details that make spaces more beautiful, more playful, and healthier for all. She is a research assistant at Harvard University's Joint Center for Housing Studies and is currently earning her Master of Architecture degree at Harvard's Graduate School of Design.

Timothy A. Schuler writes about the built and natural environments. A contributing editor at *Landscape Architecture Magazine* since 2015, his work also regularly appears in *Places Journal*, *Bloomberg CityLab*, *Metropolis*, *The Architect's Newspaper*, and *FLUX* magazine. He lives in Kansas.

Charles Shafaieh is an arts journalist and critic based in Paris. His writing on visual art, music, theater, literature, and architecture has appeared in numerous international publications, including *The New Yorker*, *The Financial Times*, *The Irish Times*, and *Artforum*.

Patrick Sisson is a Chicago expat living in Los Angeles. He writes and reports about the trends, technology, and policy that shape our cities. He has covered everything from the race to slash building emissions and drone technology in police departments to housing policy and unsung modernist architects across the US. His work has appeared in *The New York Times*, *Bloomberg CityLab*, *Vox*, and *MIT Technology Review*.

Aaron Smithson is a dual Master in Urban Planning and Master in Architecture candidate at Harvard University's Graduate School of Design. He Is a research assistant at the Joint Center for Housing Studies, and his writing has appeared in *Architectural Record*, *The Architect's Newspaper*, and *Dwell*.

Sarah M. Whiting is the Dean and Josep Lluís Sert Professor of Architecture at Harvard University's Graduate School of Design. She is also a design principal and cofounder of WW Architecture, based in Cambridge, MA.

Stephen Zacks is an advocacy journalist, architecture critic, urbanist, and project organizer based in New York City.

Mimi Zeiger is a Los Angeles-based critic, editor, and curator. She was co-curator of the US Pavilion for the 2018 Venice Architecture Biennale and co-curator of the 2020–2021 Exhibit Columbus entitled "New Middles: From Main Street to Megalopolis, What Is the Future of the Middle City?" She has written for *The New York Times*, *The Los Angeles Times*, *Architectural Review*, *Metropolis*, and *Architect*. She is an opinion columnist for *Dezeen* magazine and former West Coast editor of *The Architect's Newspaper*. Zeiger is the 2015 recipient of the Bradford Williams Medal for excellence in writing about landscape architecture.

Image Credits

The editors have attempted to secure the rights for and acknowledge all sources of images used and apologize for any errors or omissions.

Theme	Image Page	Copyright
Disguised Density	26	Iwan Baan
	28 (top)	Iwan Baan
	28 (bottom)	Here and Now Agency
	30 (top)	Andrew Welch Photography
	30 (bottom)	Lincoln Barbour Studio
	31	Eric Staudenmaier
Working with Water	40 (top)	Designed by FSY Architects, Los Angeles / Photographed by Natalia Knezevic
	40 (bottom)	Designed by FSY Architects, Los Angeles / Photographed by Natalia Knezevic
	42	Miranda Estes Photography
	44	Grant Stewart / Analogous
	46	Bill Purcell
The New Era of Amenity	57	James Ronan Architects / James Florio
	58 (top)	Albert Vecerka / Esto, Courtesy WXY architecture+urban design
	58 (bottom)	NBBJ / Cory Klein
	60	Christophe Servieres / Shot2Sell, Courtesy of Runberg Architecture Group, PLLC
Adaptive Renovations	72	Andrew Pogue
	73	Paul Turang
	74 (top)	Rory Doyle
	74 (bottom)	TCA Architects, Inc. / City Fabrick
	75 (top)	UrbanWorks and Lee Bey Photography
	75 (bottom)	Sam Oberter
	77	Sam Oberter
	79	Rafael Gamo
Creating Context	88 (top)	Pavel Bendov, Courtesy of ODA
	88 (bottom)	Pavel Bendov, Courtesy of ODA
	91	Jonathan Morefield / Field Condition
	93 (top)	Jason Keen
	93 (bottom)	Jim Innes Photography
	94	Ashwood Construction, Inc / Jeffrey Scott Agency
	95	Ashwood Construction, Inc / Jeffrey Scott Agency
Creative Corridors	104	Here and Now Agency
	106 (top)	Here and Now Agency
	106 (bottom)	Here and Now Agency
	108 (top)	Here and Now Agency
	108 (bottom)	Here and Now Agency
	109 (top)	Iwan Baan
	109 (bottom)	Iwan Baan
	111 (top)	Andrew Welch Photography
	111 (bottom)	Andrew Welch Photography